EUROPEAN HAND
FIREARMS

The Manufacture of Powder in the XVIIth Century

(Reproduced from " Travaux de Mars," published in Paris in 1685)

EUROPEAN HAND FIREARMS

OF THE SIXTEENTH, SEVENTEENTH & EIGHTEENTH CENTURIES, BY HERBERT J. JACKSON, & WITH

A TREATISE ON SCOTTISH HAND FIRE-ARMS BY CHARLES E. WHITELAW, I.A., F.S.A.Scot. MDCCCCXXIII

The Naval & Military Press Ltd

published in association with

ROYAL
ARMOURIES

Published by
The Naval & Military Press Ltd
Unit 10 Ridgewood Industrial Park,
Uckfield, East Sussex,
TN22 5QE England
Tel: +44 (0) 1825 749494
Fax: +44 (0) 1825 765701
www.naval–military-press.com

in association with

ROYAL
ARMOURIES

*In reprinting in facsimile from the original, any imperfections are inevitably reproduced
and the quality may fall short of modern type and cartographic standards.*

Printed and bound by Antony Rowe Ltd, Eastbourne

TO MY WIFE

ERRATA

P. 9, last line. *Delete* " with."

P. 13, l. 13. *For* " second" *read* " first."

P. 66, l. 13 from bottom. *After* " principle" *insert* " of."

P. 100, " ALEXANDER CAMERON." *At end of paragraph add :*
"(Plate VI, Fig. 23)."

P. 102, " IH." *For* " heart butt" *read* " scroll butt."

„ " WILLIAM HERIOT." *At end of paragraph add :*
"(Page 67, Fig. J)."

P. 104, " RM." *At end of paragraph add :* " (Plate IV, Fig. 12)."

P. 105, " THOMAS MURDOCH." *At end of paragraph add :*
"(Plate VII, Fig. 28)."

ORDER OF CONTENTS

EUROPEAN HAND FIREARMS
By H. J. Jackson

A TREATISE ON SCOTTISH FIREARMS
BY C. E. WHITELAW

INDEX OF PLATES AND FIGURES

FOREWORD

MANY books have been written treating incidentally of hand firearms of the XVIth century, and more fully of those of the XIXth century. It is my belief, however, that no book has been published in this country specially treating of firearms of the intervening period.

This is remarkable, for, whether judged from the artistic or collector's point of view, those of the XVIIth and XVIIIth centuries are unquestionably the most interesting.

During the XVIIth century fine metal-work, and especially the art of chiselling in steel, reached its zenith, and was combined with great artistic merit and elegance of design. This is proved by the barrels, locks, and furnishings of the finer weapons, many of which are veritable works of art, attracting the interest of both collectors and connoisseurs.

Those of the XVIIIth century have not the same artistic merit, but show a marked advance in the development of efficiency and fine workmanship. This period is also an attractive one to those interested in weapons having curious and ingenious mechanism.

It will, therefore, be my chief endeavour, as a collector of forty years' standing, specializing in firearms of this intervening period, to give as concise and brief a description as possible of the various types then used in Europe.

Realizing, however, the serious difficulty of conveying a correct idea by description alone, not only of the different types, but of the artistic work and beautiful designs of the furnishings, I have decided to include many illustrations, mostly reproduced from my own negatives.

Among those specimens illustrated are included a number of locks detached from pistols and guns, for from a careful study of these much may be learned.

At different periods both the form of the component parts and also of the mechanism varied considerably; and further, should a firearm be either dated or bear a gunsmith's mark, this will, with rare exceptions, be shown on the lock plate, sometimes being repeated on the barrel.

Therefore, although some conclusions may be formed from the design of the furnishings, the style of decoration, or the shape of the stock or butt, I am quite convinced that the lock, with few exceptions, is by far the surest and safest guide not only to the probable date, but also to the country of origin of the weapon.

Many of the interesting and beautiful specimens exhibited at Hertford House, the Tower of London, and other museums both here and throughout Europe, also those in the possession of large private collectors, have already been described and illustrated, and are, therefore, doubtless known to the majority of collectors. To some of these I shall occasionally refer.

The illustrations will be found at the end of each chapter in which their descriptions are given, which both for reference and comparison may be found more convenient.

Should this short work prove helpful to those interested in this subject or to any of the increasing number of collectors, the Author will be amply repaid.

The Author wishes to express his gratitude to Mr. Charles E. Whitelaw, I.A., F.S.A.Scot. (one of the greatest authorities on Scottish Hand Firearms and Weapons), for his Treatise. This he kindly agreed to write in order to complete the work.

H. J. J.

EUROPEAN HAND FIREARMS
OF THE SIXTEENTH, SEVENTEENTH, AND EIGHTEENTH CENTURIES

CHAPTER I

WHEEL- AND MATCH-LOCKS OF THE XVITH AND XVIITH CENTURIES

 SHALL not attempt to treat fully of either match- or wheel-lock weapons of the XVIth century, much having already been written on this subject. My endeavour will be to describe in this chapter the wheel-lock of the XVIIth century, giving but a brief survey of the earlier period.

The invention of the match-lock proper, namely with a spring to the serpentine, is reported to have been made very early in the XVIth century. The first idea conceived, probably early in the XVth century, had no spring to the serpentine, and could, therefore, hardly be termed a lock such as we understand it.

With this lock, ignition could only be obtained by carrying a separate flint and steel.

The wheel-lock is generally believed to have been invented in Nuremberg about 1517, and the long period during which it was used suffices to prove its efficiency. The intricate mechanism caused the production to be costly, but notwithstanding this it remained, as did the match-lock, in favour for a long time after the inventions of both the snaphaunce and flint-lock proper. It consists of a steel wheel or disc, the edge of which, grooved and serrated, protrudes through the flash pan. In the centre of this wheel a square hole is cut, enabling it to be fixed to the lock plate after passing over the square-cut spindle, to which the spanner or key is fitted. This spindle, passing through the lock plate, is attached by means of a short chain (usually of three links) to a very powerful spring. The wheel, when wound, is held by the nose of the sear, being forced (through a hole in the lock plate) to enter a cavity at the back of it, and the pyrites holder, by a spring, is made to press upon the sliding pan cover. On pulling the trigger, the sear spring is released, causing the wheel to revolve rapidly, and the pan cover to be shot back, the contact of the pyrites with the revolving wheel making sparks sufficient to fire the priming in the pan.

When first introduced this lock was a somewhat crude one, both in design and workmanship, but was much improved during the second half of the XVIth century.

The invention of the wheel-lock was an important factor in the development of the pistol, for it enabled a weapon to be carried in the holster, both primed and ready for firing.

The term fire-lock was (I think) first used to denote the wheel-lock and to distinguish this from the match-lock. There is little doubt, however, that in some cases the term was used at a later date when describing weapons fitted with flint, and also snaphaunce locks.

For the sake of comparison with later ones, it may prove interesting to give a few examples of the early types of both match- and wheel-locks.

Fig. 1 illustrates a XVth century battle-axe, the handle being a match-lock pistol, the serpentine of which, it may be noted, has no spring. This is said to have been dug up near Peterborough.

Fig. 2 shows a fine example of the later and perfected form of the European match-lock musket of the end of the XVIth century, having a spring to the serpentine and the flash pan and cover attached to the barrel. The stock of this is of fine bold form and profusely inlaid with brass wire-work, introducing quaint birds, besides having a brass shield on each side of the stock. It is further inlaid with engraved mother-of-pearl and bone. The lock is a fine and bold one, and of good workmanship.

Most of the early match-lock muskets are of considerable weight and length, the one illustrated being 5 ft. 4 in. long, and weighing over 12 lb. This necessitated the use of a forked rest, a typical example of which is here shown, being of brass finely engraved and pierced.

In Fig. 3 is illustrated an early and rare type of German wheel-lock, having two pyrites holders. Major Victor Farquharson in his collection has an exactly similar pistol lock which bears the date 1509, but without doubt the third figure is a mistake, and should read either 1, 2, or 3.

At about the end of the XVIth century a wheel-lock was invented, probably in Spain, in which both the doghead and wheel were actuated by the same spring. This very rare type of lock is shown in Fig. 4.

The artistic merit of the wheel-lock only reached its zenith during the XVIIth century, as is proved by the beautiful chiselling and design of the locks and furnishings, combined with the graceful lines of so many of the weapons of this period. The stocks of wheel-lock guns were usually straight, and very short, and considerable difficulty would have been experienced had a quick shot from the shoulder been necessary. From all accounts it would seem more than doubtful that they were ever used in the attempt to kill any but sitting game, and when used in battle by mounted men, were presumably fired from either the hip or thigh. By unmounted men a forked rest was generally used with the musket.

The high quality and artistic design of the inlay work and other decoration of the stocks are remarkable, proving firstly that no expense was spared in order to bring the completed weapon to the highest standard of artistic merit, and secondly, that the majority of those handed down to us could only have been possessed by the wealthy. The fine quality and artistic design of the inlay work and other forms of decoration on gun stocks are shown equally on those of pistols, and probably the very finest may be found on the latter. Of the cruder forms, such as those used by troops in battle, few have been preserved, owing probably to their coarse workmanship and lack of artistic merit.

A different method altogether was adopted when stocking wheel-lock pistols, for on their first introduction the stocks were made at an abrupt angle to the barrel, and usually terminated in a ball for the butt. In course of time, however, the stocks became straighter, and the butts more elongated, and the length of the pistols was increased, which improved not only the appearance but the balance. A representative specimen of the very finest type of a late XVIth century wheel-lock pistol, showing the finest workmanship of this period, is illustrated in Figs. 5 and 6.

The stock and butt are of ebony, inlaid with hunting subjects, mascaroons, etc., of engraved buckhorn and mother-of-pearl.

The butt has gilt metal ribs, terminating in a medallion in high relief, and has a chased band at the juncture with the stock.

The lock has the wheel boxed with a chased and perforated cover of metal gilt, and the lock plate shows traces of damascening.

Fig. 7 shows another typical XVIth century wheel-lock pistol of somewhat similar form, but with a safety catch on the reverse side to the lock.

The barrel is dated 1594, and both this and the lock plate bear an armourer's mark which I believe to be that of a Nuremberg gunsmith.

The so-called "dag" was a short and early form of the wheel-lock pistol, having a short flat stock, usually formed of wood inlaid, but occasionally of metal engraved, and was principally used during the second half of the XVIth century. A representative example is shown in Fig. 8, this having a stock of wood well inlaid with ivory in the best style of the period. Originally in the Meyrick collection, this pistol is now in the collection of Mr. W. H. Fenton.

The following Fig., 9, illustrates a typical petronel of the finest quality and workmanship. Petronel, a corruption of poitrinal, the name originally used by the French to describe the early bombardes, was later applied to these long, straight pistols used by cavalry at the end of the XVIth and beginning of the XVIIth century.

The one here shown is 30 inches long, the stock and pommel being well inlaid in ivory and the lock engraved in the best style with late Renaissance decoration.

The following extracts, taken from "A Treatise of Arms," being an addendum to "English Military Discipline," published by Robert Harford in 1680, will, I think, prove interesting to many. Referring to firearms, presumably of about the middle of the XVIIth century, and speaking of the musket, it states:

> The Butt of the Musket must be put to the breast half a foot below the chin.

Of Firelocks:

> With a Fire lock one may shoot juster than with a musket, because it is presented in a quite different way; that is to say, the end of the Butt to the shoulder, the side to the cheek, shutting the left eye, and aiming with the other through the sight hole, which answers to the little button on the muzzel of the barrel. Firelocks are apter to mis-give than Muskets, through the defects of the Flints and Springs.

Of the Mousqueton :

> Is not so long as the Fusil or Fire lock; nor does it by a third carry so far unless the barrel be screwed and rifled.

Of the Pistol :

> Pistols are not all of the same length nor size. The usual length of the barrels of those which are at present used among the Horse is a foot, and of stock and all a foot and a half or thereabouts.
>
> The bullet sized to the bore is five lignes in diameter, the charge a dram of powder, and it will carry forty paces, more or less, according to the goodness of the powder.

Of Carabins:

> Carabins are a kind of Fire Arms, which take their name from those ancient Souldiers, called Carabins, who commonly made use of them in the Wars. They are of two kinds, the common and the extraordinary. The common are those which were used by the King's Guard not long ago, and are usually called Carabins with great Locks; which differ in nothing as to length, size and carrying, from Fusils and Mousquetons, but only that they have Wheel-works. The extraordinary are those which the French call Arquebusses Guttières; such as are those still used by all the Arquebusiers, whose little Wheel-work is provided of a double spring for facilitating and speeding the discharge, and whose barrel, being thicker than that of common Carabins, can carry blank a thousand paces, with the same proportion of powder as is necessary for a Fusil; because it is screwed and rifled, that is to say wrought and crevassed in the inside from the muzzel to the breech in form of a screw, and from thence proceeds the justness of Arquebusses.
>
> All Carabins or Arquebusses have Wheel-works, as well those of great as small Locks, which are bent with a Spanner proportionated to the thickness of the Axel-tree of the Wheel.
>
> Heretofore were used Arquebusses, which fired with a Match, in the same manner as Muskets, but these Arms are now out of use.
>
> The King commands at present—that in every Troop of his Guards be carried eight rifled or screwed Carabins, with locks like to those of Fusils, Mousquetons and Pistols.

Before proceeding further, it may prove of interest to give a short account of the earliest inventions of breech loading, revolving, and repeating firearms. The most interesting specimens of these can only be seen in some of the museums, and in certain large private collections, most of which have already been both fully described and illustrated, leaving nothing but a brief survey necessary.

It was in the reign of Henry VIII that the breech-loading arquebus, fitted with a match-lock, was invented, as can be seen by that shown in the Tower of London, Class XII, No. 1. Similar weapons, however, of about the same date, fitted with the wheel-lock, may be seen in the Wallace Collection, the Science and Art Museum in Edinburgh, the Kennedy Collection, etc. This invention was similar to the well-known Snider action. At the commencement of the XVIth century, AUG. COTTER's name is connected with a design for a detachable breech piece for cannon, this being held in position by a transversal wedge or bolt, and ever since known as the Cotter pin. This is probably the basis and origin of the movable breech pieces afterwards applied to small arms.

Another very interesting example of the breech-loading action in the XVIth century is shown in the Tower of London, Nos. 34-42, Class V, namely, the combined shield and pistol, the latter being breech-loading with a match-lock.

As regards revolving firearms, the earliest specimen is probably the match-lock gun in the Tower of London collection, Class XII, No. 469, described as middle of the XVIth century. Other revolving guns and pistols were made with wheel-locks, but all were revolved by hand, and the mechanism was somewhat crude. It was not until 1810 that Collier invented a revolving gun and pistol which in any way corresponds with the revolver as we know it to-day.

The conception, for making a gun to fire several charges from one barrel, originated in the XVIth century, and specimens of both match- and wheel-lock arquebus may be found in museums, firing from two up to as many as eight charges from one barrel. This invention was also later adapted to flint-lock weapons. It was, however, somewhat dangerous, for the various charges were rammed one on the top of the other, there being touch-holes and pans made at certain intervals along the barrel. Weapons firing but two charges were usually fitted with two match holders or dogheads placed one behind the other, but for more, one match holder or doghead working on a rack, enabling it to be moved either forwards or backwards, was generally used. The last charge put in the barrel had necessarily to be fired first, and the match holder or doghead then brought back to the second, and so on. The manufacture of weapons of this description, although so palpably dangerous, was continued until the XVIIIth century, as will be shown in a later chapter.

It was not uncommon for the wheel-lock to be made with two pyrites holders, one being placed on each side of the wheel, so that when the pyrites in one holder became worn away, the other could be used. Also there were many double wheel-locks, that is to say, two complete locks affixed to one plate, in some cases both locks being actuated by a single trigger, but in most cases by two. Again, weapons with locks combining both the wheel and match, although very rare, are sometimes met with. At the end of the XVIIth century Marshal Vauban claimed as an invention the so-called Vauban lock, being a combination of the ordinary flint with the match-lock; but from the foregoing it may be judged to have been simply an adaptation, to the flint-lock, of a very much earlier invention. It is even said to have been used in this country some years before that date! The same idea of combination in locks was continued up to the beginning of the XIXth century, namely, flint combined with percussion, as will be shown later.

Towards the end of the XVIIth century a wheel-lock was invented (probably in Germany) with a geared wheel, and it is extraordinary that so important an improvement should not have been discovered earlier.

It is only possible to give a few illustrations of representative specimens of wheel-locks of the XVIIth century, which it is hoped may suffice to give some idea of the various types and beautiful workmanship.

Figs. 10 and 11 show the exterior and interior views of a rare type of combination wheel- and match-lock, being a fine specimen, probably made in Germany during the early part of the XVIIth century, and Figs. 12 and 13 the exterior and interior views of an interesting and rare type of double wheel-lock, of either the end of the XVIth or very early XVIIth century. This lock, fired by a single trigger, has two sears connected loosely by a chain. The first pull on the trigger actuates one sear, thus firing the first lock; and the second pull, by tightening the chain, actuates the second sear, and so fires the second lock. The invention, therefore, of the single-trigger gun was made some 200 years earlier than is generally believed.

Fig. 14 illustrates a fine specimen of a Brescian lock of the first half of the XVIIth century, having two pyrites holders, one on each side of the wheel, and is on the same principle as that shown in Fig. 3.

The reason for this invention was to insure the discharge, should the pyrites in one doghead either break or fail from any cause to ignite the powder in the pan. The second doghead could then be used, thus preventing the delay caused by having to fix fresh pyrites to the holder. Single locks of this type were those commonly used in Italy at this time.

In Figs. 15 and 16 are given two illustrations showing each side of a quite exceptionally fine specimen of an Italian wheel-lock pistol of about the middle of the XVIIth century, which, although not marked, is without doubt the work of Lazarino Cominazzo. This weapon, 22 inches long, is a fine example of the perfection of workmanship and design and proves the high efficiency attained by the Cominazzo family, both in the chiselling and in the elaborate piercing of the steel. It further shows the beautiful steel lacelike work so often used in mounting these fine weapons. The butt and trigger guard are most beautifully and elaborately pierced, as well as chiselled, and the graceful lines and general finish could not be surpassed.

In order to demonstrate more clearly the highly artistic treatment of the decoration and exquisite quality of the chiselling and piercing of the furnishings, an enlarged illustration of the butt end of this pistol is shown in Fig. 17.

Fig. 18 illustrates a typical pair of the smaller wheel-lock pistols of about the same period. These are $15\frac{3}{4}$ inches long and marked on the barrel LAZARI COMINAZ.

The mounts are well chiselled in the best Brescian style, and the workmanship and finish of the locks are of the finest.

The following Fig., 19, illustrates an exceptionally fine and bold pair of wheel-lock pistols, $20\frac{1}{2}$ inches long. The only mark on these is D.B. on the interior of the lock plate, from which they may be assumed to be the work of Domenico Bonomino of Brescia.

The quality and design of the furnishings and locks, combined with the graceful lines of these pistols, may be considered almost equal to those by Lazarino Cominazzo. It should be noted that the barrels are octagonal in form from breech to muzzle, which, at this period, is quite unusual. The sash hooks, of beautiful form, are also worthy of notice.

By the kind permission of Mr. W. H. Fenton I am also able to illustrate in Fig. 20 an exceptionally fine example of a detached Brescian wheel-lock. The chiselling of this lock is in the best Brescian style, and the artistic design perfect. It is without doubt the work of the Cominazzo family, and probably the only part remaining of what must have been a beautiful weapon.

The following entry in Evelyn's "Diary" early in 1646 is interesting:

> We came this evening to Brescia, which next morning we traverst, according to our custom, in search of antiquities and new sights. Here I purchased of old Lazarino Cominazzo my fine carabine, which cost me 9 pistoles, this City being famous for these firearms, and that workman with Jo Bap Franco, the best esteemed.

It may be assumed from Evelyn speaking of "old" Cominazzo that he had then been established for many years.

In Fig. 21 is shown a wheel-lock sporting gun, the stock elaborately inlaid with figures and animals in brass, and with brass wire scrollwork. The trigger guard and other mounts are also of brass, and the length is 46 inches. This has no mark, but is probably Dutch, of about the middle of the XVIIth century.

Figs. 22 and 23 illustrate a fine example of a late German wheel-lock gun, having a well-chiselled lock and barrel, the stock being covered with ivory, elaborately engraved with hunting scenes. This is 38½ inches long, and probably dates from about the middle of the XVIIth century.

In Fig. 24 the finely engraved and interesting German lock with a geared wheel is shown, being the late XVIIth century one already referred to.

It may be of interest to illustrate a few typical XVIth century powder flasks, primers, spanners, and a patron, and to compare these with representative examples of those of the XVIIth century.

In Fig. 25 is shown a very fine example of steel patron of the XVIth century (probably Italian) to hold four cartridges. These cartridges, covered with paper, were adopted in order to shorten the process of loading, for by biting off the end, the charge could be rammed home, leaving it only necessary to prime the pan before firing. In Fig. 26 are shown three typical spanners used for winding with the wheel-lock, the middle one of which is a combined spanner and primer. Figs. 27 and 28 illustrate two XVIth century powder flasks and a primer—Fig. 27 being a fine specimen of an Italian ivory flask, well carved and mounted, and Fig. 28 a metal flask, of fine form, and a primer; the latter, heavily gilt, is dated 1573.

The following three plates show different types of powder flasks used during the XVIIth century. Fig. 29 is formed of wood with steel mounts, and has the original cord. This probably is English, of the early part of the century. Fig. 30 is a fine example of a German flask formed of a tusk of ivory, well carved with a hunting scene. Fig. 31, formed of pear wood, finely carved with deer- and boar-hunting episodes, and beautifully mounted in silver, is probably Flemish, of about the middle of the century.

There are many other specimens of this period, which I would like to illustrate, but those given may be considered characteristic.

PLATE I

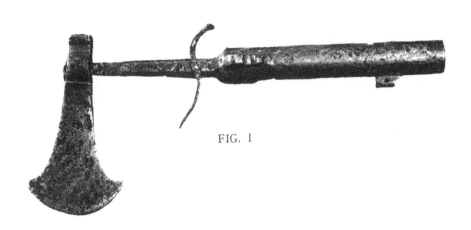

FIG. I

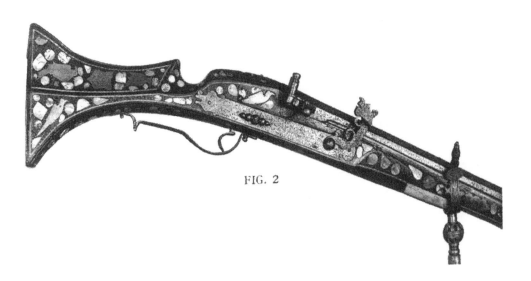

FIG. 2

PLATE II

FIG. 3

FIG. 4

PLATE III

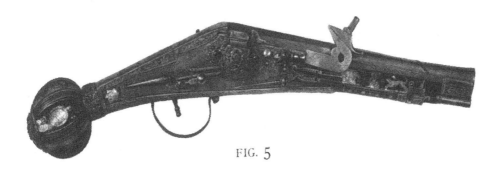

FIG. 5

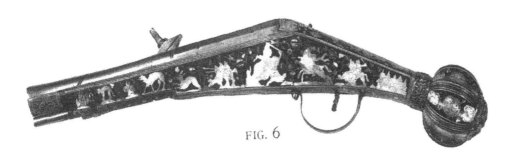

FIG. 6

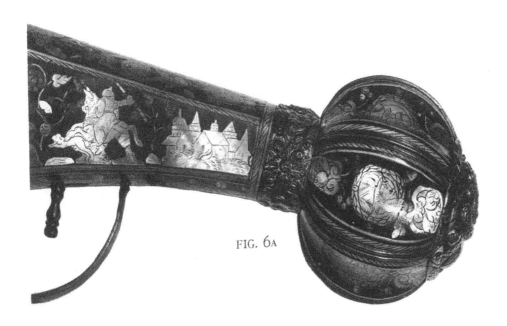

FIG. 6A

PLATE IV

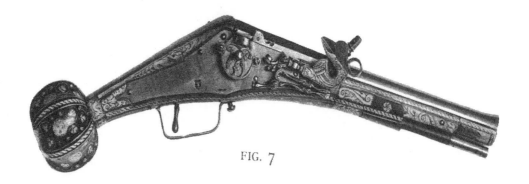

FIG. 7

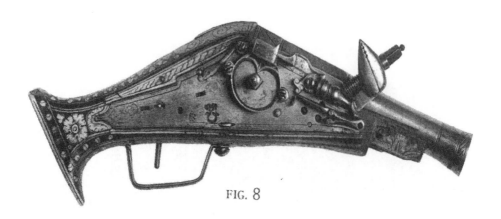

FIG. 8

PLATE V

FIG. 9

FIG. 10

FIG. 11

PLATE VI

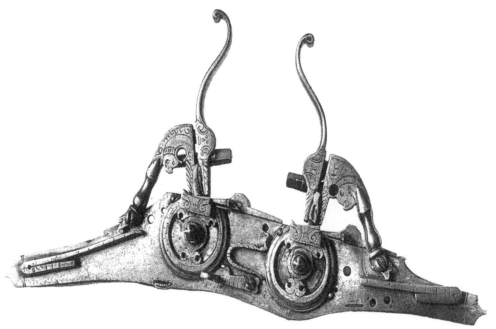

FIG. 12

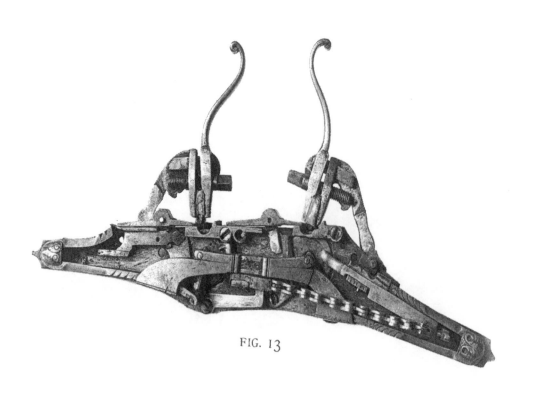

FIG. 13

PLATE VII

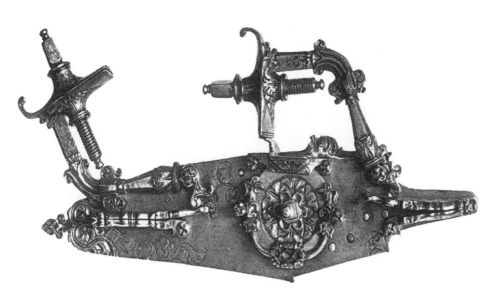

FIG. 14

PLATE VIII

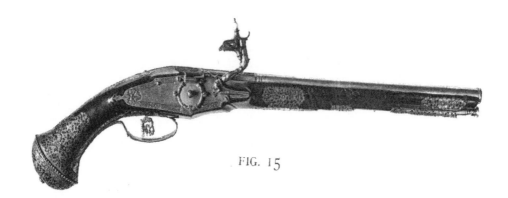

FIG. 15

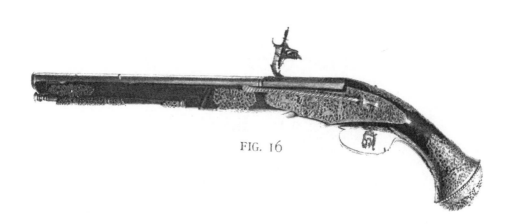

FIG. 16

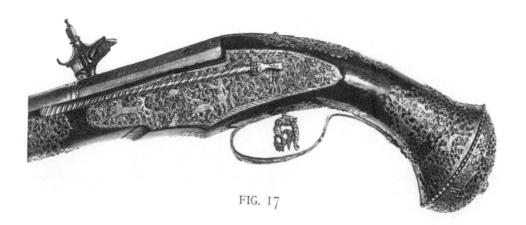

FIG. 17

PLATE IX

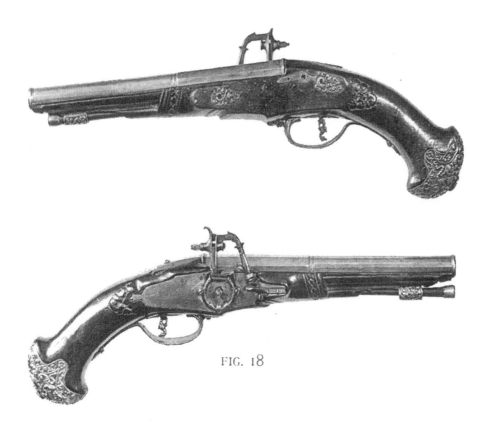

FIG. 18

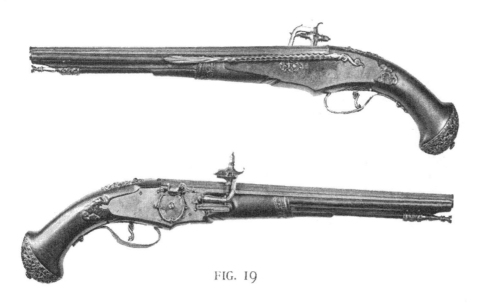

FIG. 19

PLATE X

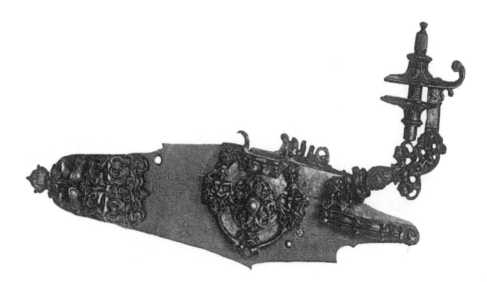

FIG. 20

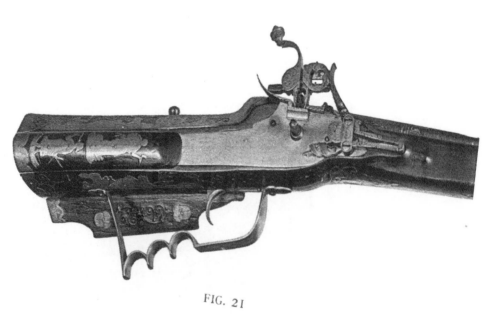

FIG. 21

PLATE XI

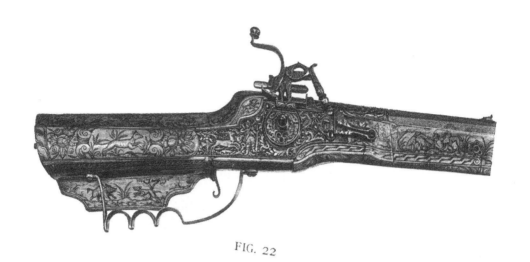

FIG. 22

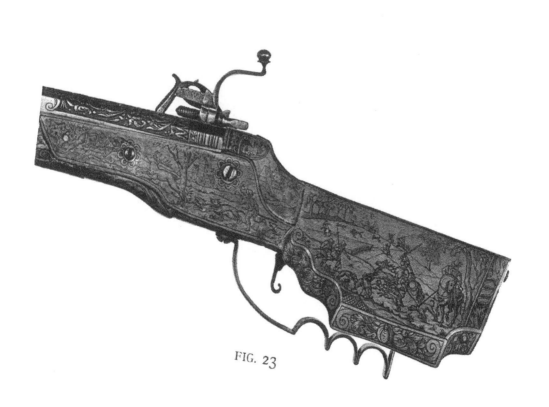

FIG. 23

PLATE XII

FIG. 24

PLATE XIII

FIG. 25

PLATE XIV

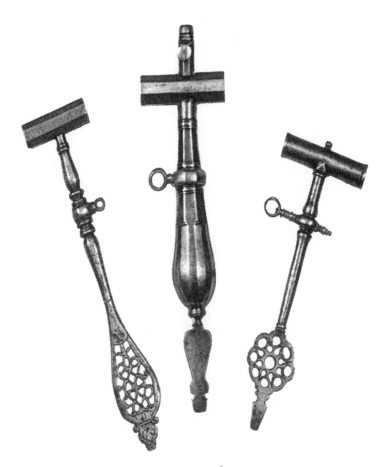

FIG. 26

PLATE XV

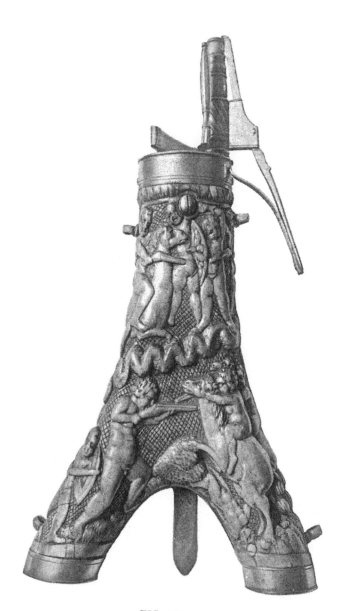

FIG. 27

PLATE XVI

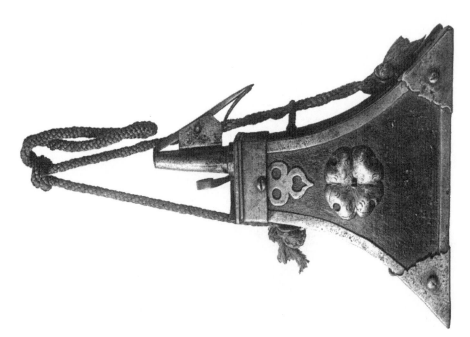

FIG. 29

FIG. 28

PLATE XVII

FIG. 30

PLATE XVIII

FIG. 31

CHAPTER II

Snaphaunce and Transition Weapons and Locks

T has been previously mentioned that the wheel-lock continued in favour for a long period (probably about 150 years) after the invention and introduction of the snaphaunce lock.

This was invented about the middle of the XVIth century, but the country of origin is uncertain. The earliest examples handed down to us are either Spanish, Scotch, or German, and the invention is generally supposed to have emanated from Spain.

It was more or less superseded in 1630 by the invention of the flint-lock (proper), the more simple mechanism of which made its production less costly.

The period, therefore, during which the snaphaunce lock was in favour is a short one, and probably accounts for the fact that they are rarer to-day than any other type of weapon. Most specimens are now either in museums or some of the larger private collections.

The snaphaunce retains the sliding pan cover of the wheel-lock, and differs in this respect from the flint-lock. Further, the steel is fixed to a movable arm, and entirely disconnected from the pan cover, whereas in flint-locks the steel and pan cover are in one piece. The fall of the doghead causes the pan cover (actuated by a spring on the inside of the lock plate) to slide forward and so to uncover the flash pan.

The term "snaphaunce" is erroneously applied by some writers to the form of flint-lock of the early Spanish type.

The derivation of this term is, by some, attributed to the Dutch "snaphanns" meaning "chicken thieves," although I think the more likely derivation to be the German "Schappehahn" meaning "pecking fowl." This lock is said to have been invented, and at first used by thieves and marauders, the expensive wheel-lock being beyond their means, and the match-lock (with its lighted match) too risky and dangerous for use on their excursions.

Probably the earliest remaining examples are a pair of Scottish pistols in the museum of Dresden, the locks of which are on the snaphaunce principle. These are dated 1598.

The early Spanish form of this lock is probably that illustrated in Fig. 32. Unfortunately, however, this is not dated.

Another early form (probably English) is that shown in the following Fig., 33.

Very interesting examples may be seen in the Tower of London. In Class XII, No. 736, is a pistol (described as of the middle of the XVIth century), the lock of which is the earliest form of snaphaunce. This is German and bears the Nuremberg mark.

In the same collection, Class XII, Nos. 63 and 737, are to be seen two other early specimens, the former being the "birding piece" of Charles I, dated 1614, and the latter, a pistol dated 1619.

Although not the earliest, by far the most beautiful snaphaunce weapons, combining the finest of workmanship with artistic decoration and elegance of design, were made in Italy (chiefly at Brescia) about the middle of the XVIIth century, at which time the art of chiselling in steel was brought as near to perfection as possible. Doubtless, the finest examples are the work of the Cominazzo family and their apprentices, who for two or three generations from the commencement of the century held the highest reputation for the artistic craftsmanship of the firearms they produced.

Spain held the second place, some of the Spanish workmanship and chiselling being of a very high standard. They were never able to reach, however, the perfection attained by Brescia, nor did their weapons show the same elegance of design.

It is impossible to say when the snaphaunce was first used in our army, but certainly early in the XVIIth century.

Lord Strafford states in a despatch from Ireland, presumably about 1633: "Among 13092 men, 7226 swords, 8083 pikes, 700 muskets, 384 calivers, 836 snaphaunces, 69 halberts, 11 lances"; and Cromwell in 1651, also from Ireland, writes: "We have left us in store but four hundred pair of pistols, two thousand and thirty muskets, whereof thirty snaphaunces."

The following illustrations are representative of some of the finer quality of snaphaunce locks and firearms, the cruder form of which, although rare, would hardly find the same interest with collectors.

Fig. 34 shows an early and most interesting specimen of a double snaphaunce lock. This is the property of Mr. W. H. Fenton, who has kindly allowed me to illustrate it. It is probably German.

In the following Fig., 35, is illustrated another lock of a similar type but of Italian origin and of rather a later date. These double snaphaunce locks are of great rarity and were used with double-barrel (under and over) guns.

Fig. 36 shows a somewhat crude but early type of a single Italian snaphaunce lock.

Figs. 37 and 38 illustrate an exceptionally fine sporting gun of the second half of the XVIIth century. This is marked Lazarino Cominazzo, and the furnishings and lock are all most beautifully and elaborately chiselled and pierced in the finest Brescian style and finish. The fore part of the stock is mounted in the same style, the terminal to the ramrod being a monkey chiselled in steel. The balance of this weapon is perfect.

The following Fig., 39, shows the lock of this gun and the perfection in the art of deep chiselling attained in Brescia during the first half of the XVIIth century.

In Fig. 40 is shown an exceptionally fine pair of Brescian pistols, the chiselling of the mounts, barrels, and locks being of the finest quality. The stocks are also beautifully carved.

Fig. 41 illustrates a very fine example of an Italian lock showing great artistic merit, but the chiselling is less deep than that shown in Fig. 39.

In the next Fig., 42, is given a fine example of a snaphaunce lock made in Dusseldorf by A. Bongarde, evidently a French gunsmith domiciled there. Although unquestionably a fine example of artistic chiselling it does not favourably compare with the Brescian work either in artistic merit, quality of workmanship, or design.

In Fig. 43 is shown an early and rare form of lock which, although not the true type of snaphaunce, is very similar. Unlike the snaphaunce the steel is attached to the top of the pan cover by a screw swivel. When the doghead falls to a certain angle the pan cover flies back, but not before the pyrites strikes the steel.

This interesting lock is illustrated at full cock in order to show the extraordinary angle of the doghead, from which it might be excusable to think that the pyrites could not strike the face of the steel truly, but such is not the case.

Very interesting specimens of what may be called locks of the transition period are occasionally met with. These have lock plates resembling those of the wheel-lock, and were evidently made before the ordinary form of flint-lock had been firmly established.

Figs. 44 and 45 illustrate two of these, and Fig. 46 the interior view of the latter, which shows the mechanism to be quite exceptional, if not unique.

PLATE XIX

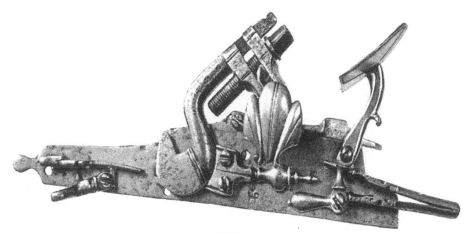

FIG. 32

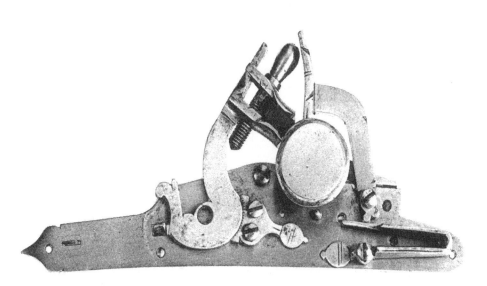

FIG. 33

PLATE XX

FIG. 34

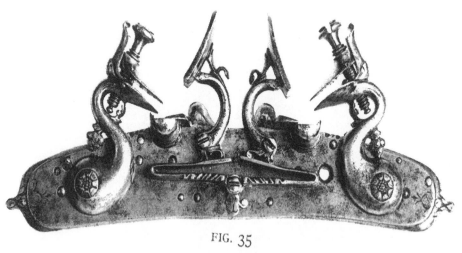

FIG. 35

FIG. 36

PLATE XXI

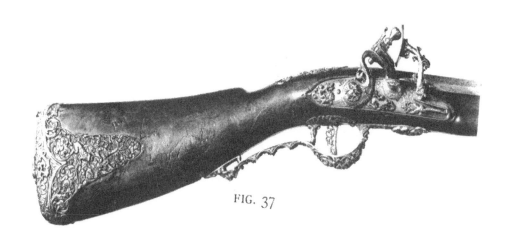

FIG. 37

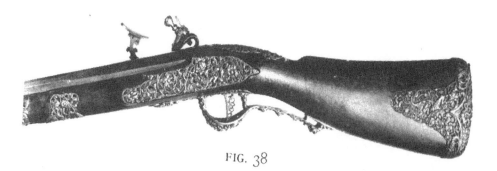

FIG. 38

FIG. 39

PLATE XXII

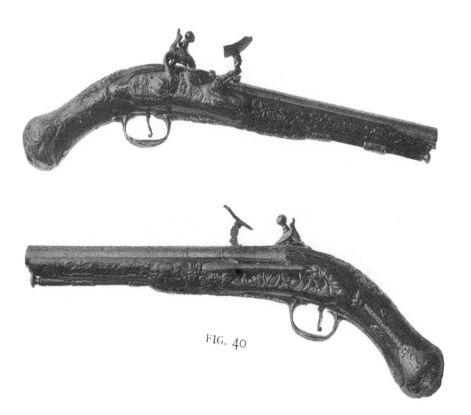

FIG. 40

PLATE XXIII

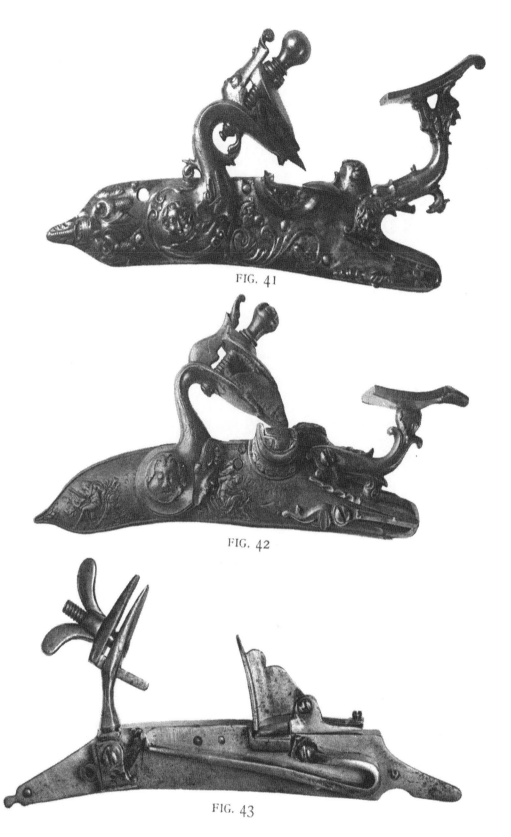

FIG. 41

FIG. 42

FIG. 43

PLATE XXIV

FIG. 44

FIG. 45

FIG. 46

CHAPTER III

The Flint-lock in the XVIIth Century

ALTHOUGH the flint-lock proper is said to have been invented in Spain about 1630, I must confess my inability to discover, either in museums or private collections, any weapon of quite so early a date fitted with this form of lock.

The earliest form of flint-lock (although an early adaptation by the Italians of the Spanish invention) is probably that shown by a drawing in permanent black ink, in Antonio Petrini's "Manuscript Treatise" on making arms and armour, etc., written in 1642. This manuscript, which I have seen, is now in the Tower of London, having been transferred there in 1914 from the library of the Patent Office. In the "Inventory and Survey of the Armouries of the Tower of London," by Mr. Charles Ffoulkes, the drawing of this lock, the date of which is probably 1635, is reproduced on page 90. It should be noted that although the mainspring is on the outside of the lock plate, it has not the same action as those found on all Spanish locks.

At about the time when this manuscript was written, Italy was producing many of her finest weapons fitted with flint-locks, and it will be found that, with few exceptions, those made in Northern Italy have the mainspring fitted on the inside of the lock plate, whereas those of Southern Italy, favouring the Spanish system, have the mainspring on the outside.

It is not difficult, however, to distinguish the Spanish from the Southern Italian lock. In all Spanish locks it will be found that the upper part of the mainspring extends beyond, and presses upwards, against the base of the doghead, the fall being thus caused by an upward pressure, whereas in Southern Italian locks it is the downward pressure of the mainspring upon the forepart of the base of the doghead which causes the fall. What I have attempted to explain will be the more readily understood by comparing the Spanish and Southern Italian locks respectively shown in Figs. 51 and 61.

With few exceptions, all other European flint-locks, both of early and late types, have the mechanism, including the mainspring, placed on the inside of the lock plate.

During the XVIIth century the Spaniards competed keenly with Italy, not only in the fine quality of the chiselling and beautiful design of the locks and furnishings fitted to their weapons, but especially in the art of barrel making. Although unable to equal them in the former, they did so in the latter, and before long obtained such a reputation for their barrels as to create a world-wide demand.

During this time, in Germany, the wheel- and match-locks continued in favour, and it would appear that neither Germany nor France seriously adopted the flint-lock until considerably later.

In England we were apparently content to import the finest of our hand firearms, and, until the latter part of the century, made no serious attempt to produce weapons of the finest quality.

This, however, does not apply to Scotland, where the manufacture of the Scottish form of pistol was started in about the latter part of the XVIth century by Caddell at Doune, in Stirlingshire, who held the highest reputation for the fine quality, design, and workmanship of these weapons. For the remainder of this century, and the following one, the trade was carried on by his descendants and John Campbell.

During the century many new inventions are reputed to have been made, but in most cases were only improvements of earlier ideas. In the first place, the early conception of a revolving weapon was improved upon, and although still revolved by hand, the mechanism and workmanship were less crude. A good specimen may be seen in the Birmingham Museum, having three barrels with one common flash pan, the spring catch for retaining the barrels in position being released by pressing the trigger with the doghead down.

Breech-loading flint-lock weapons with the barrel dropping on a hinged joint, and the charge contained in a metal cartridge, were also invented during this period, as well as some ingenious mechanisms for the fitting of magazine primers.

During the first half of the century the so-called "dog-lock" was invented, and used in this country in 1647, as is proved by the dated English lock shown in Fig. 49. The invention was a good one, for this simple form of safety catch made the fall of the doghead impossible. It was, however, eventually more used in eastern countries than in Europe.

From an artistic point of view the beauty of the design, decoration, and workmanship of the firearms of the XVIIth century were never excelled.

On the following pages will be found a list of some of the leading gun-smiths of the XVIIth century, which, however, cannot be presumed to be in any way complete, and doubtless there are many omissions. These names are taken partly from works already published, but in many cases from fire-arms in the various museums and collections.

It may also prove of interest to give two facsimiles of the names and marks of the Spanish gunsmiths of Madrid from 1684 to 1795, taken from "Compendio Historico de les Arcabuceros de Madrid," written in 1795 by Isidro Soler, himself a gunsmith. In the following chapter a few of the most interesting and representative examples of XVIIth century flint-lock weapons are described and illustrated.

CHAPTER IV

XVIIth Century Gunsmiths

ENGLAND AND SCOTLAND

T. Addis
J. Alison
Jacob Austen
Bankes
W. Bourne
Brooke
R. Burrows
Thomas Caddell and descendants
Clarkson
H. Crips
W. Dawsten
Fisher

Gorgo at London
W. Graves
Gregory
A. Hall
Hawkins
A. Hill
Koster
McKen
Moore
H. Martin Muler
J. Norcott
John Pasmore
Peddell

Theophilus Richards
Henry Rowland
Andrew Scott
Daniel Stewart
Andrew Strahan
E. Tilly
Truelock
W. Turvey
J. Watson
T. West
R. Weston

FRANCE

Pierre Bevier
Armand Bougarde
Bourgeois
Jean Caillovel
Nicholas Colas
De la Collombe
François Duclos
Jacque de Goulet

Jean de Goulet.
Gabriel
Haber
Antoine Jacquard
D. Jumeau
La Roche
François Lecourreur
François Marcou

Martin Mazue
Bertrand Piraube
Louis Renard
Jean Simonin
Claude Thomas
Thuraine

ITALY

F. Albergotti
Battazanti
E. Bianchi
Lorenso Caffi
Ventura Cani
G. Catane
Francini
Giov. Batt. Francino
Antonio Francino

Maffeo Badile
Boia
Antonio Bonisolo
Domenico Bonomino
Maffia
Marchetti
Lorenzo Comminazzo
Lazarino Cominazzo
Bartolomeo Cotel

Diomede
Antonio Petrini
Battistini Paratici
Giovanni Gavacciolo
E. Lazarino
Lazaro Lazarino
Maffeo
Raphael Verdiani

SPAIN

Simon Marcuarte
Juan Salado
Francisco Fernandez
Juan de Metola
Juan Sanchez de Miruena
Christoval de Ricla
Gaspar Fernandez

Juan Belen
Pedro Munoz
Domingo Garcia
Nicolas Bis
Alonso Martinez
Luis Santos
Juan Fernandez
Diego Esquivel

Diego Ventura
Juan Santos
Matias Baeza
Sagun
Micerguillo
Pedro Palacios

GERMANY

Berech
Johann Entzinger
Joh. Georg Erttel
H. Caspar Escher
Georg Fehr
F. J. Frey
Nikolaus Fichtner
Michael Grienvalt
Michael Gull
Caspar Keiser

Klett
Kuchenreuter
M. Linck
Matl
Franz Matzenkopf
Hans Mentel
Hans Morgenroth
Johann Neureiter
Ontner
Johann Oberlander

Joseph Piermair
Andrea Prantner
Martin Qualek
Caspar Recknagel
Rewer
Elias Schinzel
Johann Schwenck
E. G. Siaens
Johann Sommer
Hans Stockmann

GERMANY—continued

Johann Steinweg	Max Wenger	C. Wolf
Hans Stifter	Felix Werder	Andreas Zaruba
Martin Sussebecker	Franz Weyer	Markus Zilli

SWEDISH, DANISH, FLEMISH, DUTCH

Claus Dam	Heinrich Kapell	Peter Starbus
Claude Hiquet	Johann Koch	Tommer
L. M. Kalthoff	Andreas Neidhart	
Peter Kalthoff	Jacobus van Oppy	

PLATE XXV

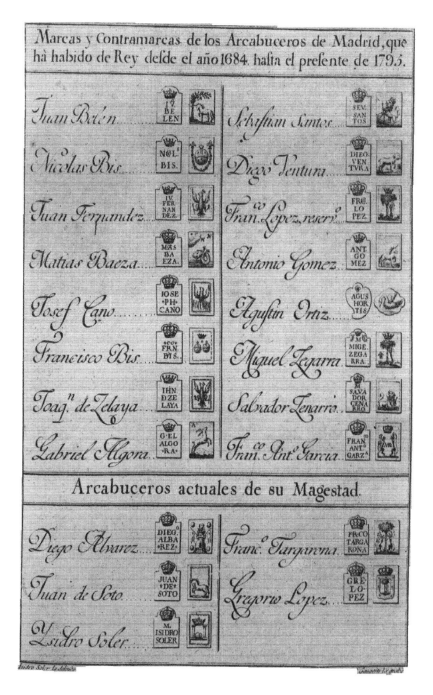

Facsimile of the names and marks of the
Gunsmiths of Madrid from 1684 to 1795 given in
"Compendio Historico de los Arcabuceros de Madrid"

Written in 1795 by Isidro Soler

PLATE XXVI

Facsimile of the names and marks of the
Gunsmiths of Madrid from 1684 to 1795 given in
"Compendio Historico de los Arcabuceros de Madrid"
Written in 1795 by Isidro Soler

CHAPTER V

Types of XVIIth Century Flint-lock Weapons

IN this chapter it is my intention only to illustrate and describe such fine or rare specimens as may be considered representative of the high standard of art and craft attained by the leading gunsmiths of Europe during the XVIIth century. By so doing it is hoped to convey some knowledge of the characteristic form of decoration and varying types produced by the different nations.

As previously remarked, England abstained from serious competition, and was apparently at this period content to import her finest arms. She even did not discourage foreign gunsmiths from establishing themselves over here. For instance, in Fig. 47 is shown a most interesting and probably unique pair of pistols which are marked on the lower part of the lock plate GORGO. AT LONDON. The maker of these, to judge from the decorative design, was doubtless of Italian descent, and probably domiciled in London during the second half of the XVIIth century. These pistols fire three separate discharges from one barrel, the breech block (over which the rifled barrel screws) containing three chambers, each of which, having a separate touch hole, is fired by a common lock, steel, and pan. By an upward pressure of the trigger guard, the catch, retaining the breech block in position, is released, enabling the breech block and barrel to be revolved by hand, thus bringing the touch hole of each chamber in turn to the flash pan, where it is held by a spring bolt. A lock of these pistols, illustrated in Fig. 48, shows the magazine primer, which, actuated by a lever attached to the steel, deposits after each discharge sufficient powder in the pan to fire the next. The length of these pistols is 19 inches, the butts, escutcheons, and furnishings being of steel finely chiselled. I have never ventured to fire these, but it would seem that a considerable quantity of gas must escape before the ball can reach the bore.

In Fig. 49 is shown the English dog-lock referred to in the previous chapter. This is dated 1647 and bears the maker's mark : H. CRIPS.

In the following Fig., 50, is given an example of the later form in use at the end of the century.

In Fig. 51 a fine specimen is shown of a well-chiselled and designed early Spanish gun-lock of about the middle of the XVIIth century. The chiselling, although fine, hardly equals the best Brescian work of the period, either in finish or execution, although it cannot be denied that the artistic design is of a high order. Fig. 52 shows a similar Spanish lock of a rather different type, the chiselling being also of fine quality. In Fig. 53 is given an illustration of the breech end of a Spanish gun barrel, which is a fine example of probably the highest standard reached by Spain in the art of chiselling in steel.

Fig. 54 illustrates a pair of Spanish pistols of an early type, having ball butts. These have no mark, but the barrels and locks are of fine workmanship, and the brass furnishings well engraved. Fig. 55 shows another unmarked and early pair of Spanish pistols, of a rare type, having short gun-shaped stocks. These have very pronounced bell-mouthed barrels, and the chiselled locks are of good design. The stocks are entirely overlaid with silver lacework roughly engraved, the trigger guards being also of silver.

In Fig. 56 are illustrated what I believe to be unique specimens of a XVIIth century knife and fork. These, although more or less freaks, are nevertheless most interesting examples of German craft, the small locks and weapons themselves being of exceptional quality and workmanship. It will be seen that miniature flint-lock pistols form the handles, and that when used these would be hidden by the hands. We may be thankful that posterity has failed to adopt such an idea as that of inviting a friend to dinner with the fixed determination that it shall be his last meal. When firing, the grip is either the blade of the knife or the prongs of the fork, neither of which can be considered ideal. The handles containing the barrels are well engraved and bear the mark, F. H. RICHTE. A. REEHE. BERG., the total length of these weapons being 8½ inches.

I will now give some examples of Italian workmanship, which, at this period, is generally acknowledged to be unequalled either for the quality of its execution or perfection of design.

In Fig. 57 is illustrated the butt end of an early Italian flint-lock sporting rifle of exceptionally artistic and graceful form. The stock is beautifully inlaid with late Renaissance decoration in engraved ivory and mother-of-pearl introducing quaint animals of the chase.

A Spanish lock of early date is fitted to this, but whether or not this is the original, it is not possible to say.

It is, however, not at all uncommon to find Spanish barrels fitted to Italian weapons.

In Fig. 58 is shown a very beautiful example of an early flint-lock for a pistol with two barrels (under and over), and also the trigger guard for same. This is doubtless the work of the Brescian family of Cominazzo of about the middle of the century, and no finer example could be given of the exquisite quality and boldness of their chiselling and design.

Fig. 59 illustrates an early type of Brescian pistol having the flattened form of butt. All the mounts, including the lock, are chiselled in the best Brescian style, the latter being of a very rare type. The barrel, grooved and chevroned, is marked LAZARO LAZARINO; and the lock, LORENZO DE STEFANI REFRONTO.

The length of this pistol is $17\frac{1}{2}$ inches.

Fig. 60 illustrates another early type of Brescian flint-lock pistol with a flattened butt. This is another example of the work of the Cominazzo family, and the barrel bears their name, but the chiselling, although good, is not of the finest quality. It is interesting, however, as showing the form of butt and exceptional length ($20\frac{1}{2}$ inches) of some of the pistols of this period.

In Fig. 61 is given a very fine example of a detached lock of a rather later period marked GIUSSEPPI GUARDIANI ANGHIAN.

This represents a somewhat different type of Italian art, and it will be noted that the chiselling is neither so bold nor so deep as that of Brescia. It nevertheless is of superb quality and has great artistic merit.

In the next Fig., 62, is shown a very beautiful pair of Brescian pistols $19\frac{1}{2}$ inches long, the barrels bearing the name LAZARINO COMINAZZO, and the lock plates PIETRO FLORENTINO. The barrels are grooved and chevroned, and the furnishings and locks are of steel, beautifully chiselled, with late

Renaissance decoration introducing figures, scrollwork, etc., in the best Brescian style. The terminals to the ramrods are monkeys chiselled in steel. These pistols, probably made about 1635, are perfect examples of Cominazzo's finest work at this time.

In order to show the exquisite quality and artistic design of the chiselling of the furnishings, an enlarged illustration of the butt end of one of these pistols is given in Fig. 63.

In Fig. 64 is illustrated a fine pair of Italian pistols of even a later date (probably quite the end of the XVIIth century). It will be seen that the chiselling on these is poor in comparison with those specimens already described, nor have they the same elegance of design. The barrels are marked LAZARI COMINAZO, but I am inclined to believe from the design of the lock, coupled with the inferior quality of chiselling and workmanship, that these were not made in Brescia, but probably in Southern Italy, being a poor attempt to copy the work of the famous Cominazzo family. The length is 15¼ inches.

Before closing this chapter it may prove interesting to give an illustration of an early Italian lock of the plainer and simpler form (Fig. 65). This does not compare from an artistic point of view with those already described, but probably represents the ordinary form of Southern Italian lock more generally in use, for it could only be the wealthy who were able to acquire the finest Brescian weapons.

PLATE XXVII

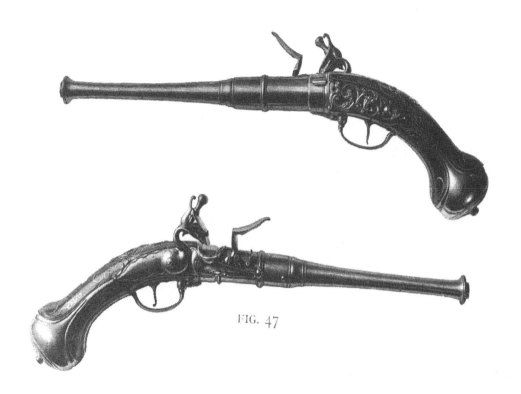

FIG. 47

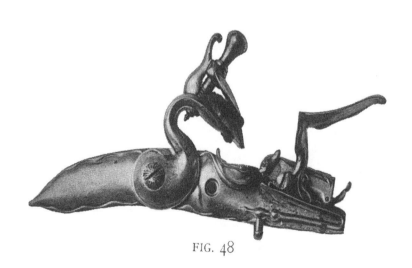

FIG. 48

PLATE XXVIII

FIG. 49

FIG. 50

PLATE XXIX

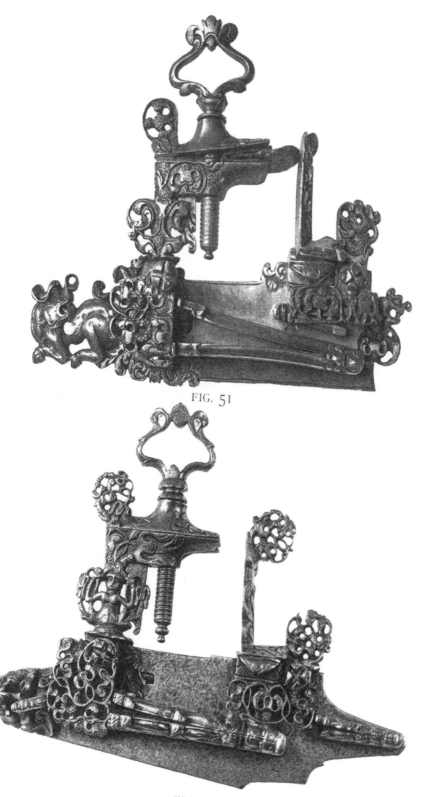

FIG. 51

FIG. 52

PLATE XXX

FIG. 53

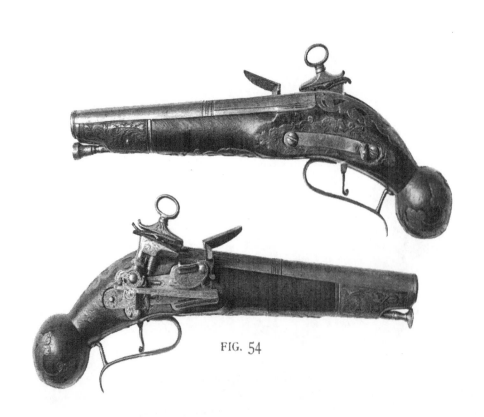

FIG. 54

PLATE XXXI

FIG. 55

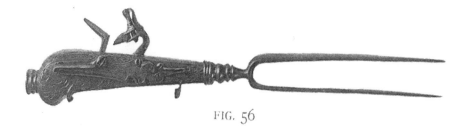

FIG. 56

PLATE XXXII

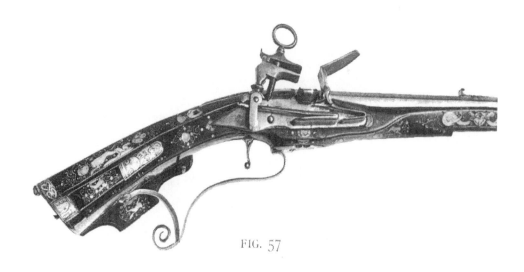

FIG. 57

FIG. 58

PLATE XXXIII

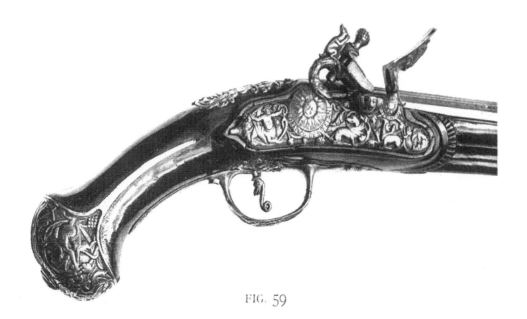

FIG. 59

PLATE XXXIV

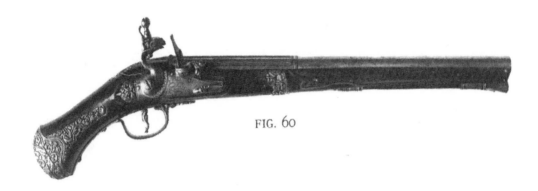

FIG. 60

FIG. 61

PLATE XXXV

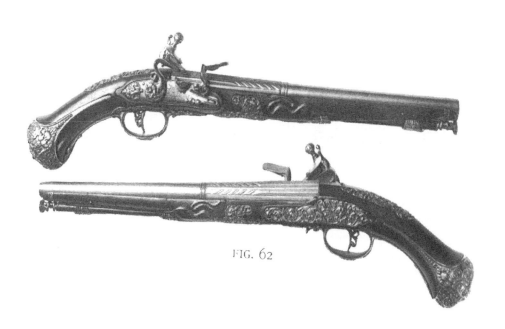

FIG. 62

FIG. 63

PLATE XXXVI

FIG. 64

FIG. 65

CHAPTER VI

THE FLINT-LOCK OF THE FIRST HALF OF THE XVIIITH CENTURY

THE earlier part of this century witnessed some changes in the form of both guns and pistols, with the object of improving their efficiency and precision, but the mechanism of the lock remained the same. In guns, the tendency on the average was towards shortening the barrels and lengthening the stocks, thus giving a better balance, and at the same time making them more serviceable for quick and accurate shooting. As the century advanced, the stocks of pistols were more curved towards the butt, and the barrels shortened, which improved both the grip and balance. On the other hand, the artistic and elaborate decoration and graceful lines of the weapons gradually deteriorated, and certainly from this point of view they do not favourably compare with those of the preceding century. It is true that some of the finest weapons, and particularly those produced by Italy and France, retained much of their former richness of decoration combined with elegance of design, but even these failed in many ways to equal those of the previous century, and more especially in the quality and execution of the chiselling. It may safely be asserted that, with the exception of Scottish pistols, the majority of both guns and pistols of this period were mounted and furnished in a much more simple and less elaborate style.

Shortly after the commencement of this century English gunsmiths began seriously to compete with those of the Continent, and before long secured a high reputation both for efficiency, excellence of quality, and fine workmanship. They, however, refrained from attempting to compete with the highly artistic and elaborate decoration of Continental weapons, but nevertheless from that time to the present, have more than held their own against the world.

With the exception of the improvements already mentioned, there is nothing of interest to note in the guns of this period.

During the early part of the century, however, an entirely new type of both holster and pocket pistol was introduced, having cannon-shaped barrels and curved stocks, the latter showing an accentuated increase in circumference towards the butt, which was usually capped with a grotesque silver mask or plain silver.

These pistols were a distinct improvement on previous types in several ways. First the barrel, by means of a key, could be unscrewed near the breech, enabling a ball fractionally larger than the bore to be placed in the barrel, and the powder in the chamber, thus insuring more accurate loading. Secondly, in some cases the barrel, when unscrewed, was held by a ring fastened by a swivel attachment to the under part of the breech block, which enabled the barrel to be folded backwards and the pistols to be more easily carried. Thirdly, this type showed an improvement both in grip and balance, and, with but slight alterations, remained in favour throughout Europe until about the middle of the second half of this century.

In the earliest type the lock, action, and barrel were in one piece, the lock being at the side, but within probably the course of only a few years the locks were made separate and fastened to the side by means of screws passing through the stock. Then, towards the middle of the century, the cock was placed in the centre of the action, and the pan, steel, and touch hole in the centre of the breech block, thus obscuring the line of sight, which one would think could hardly be termed an improvement. In most cases the stocks were elaborately and artistically decorated with silver wire inlay, and with few exceptions retained the silver mask as butt cap.

Another rare and very interesting form of this type of pistol was also introduced at about the beginning of this century, the stocks and butts (as in most Scotch pistols) being entirely of metal.

It must also be remarked that some of the finest Scotch pistols were made at this time, the artistic decoration of many being of the highest merit.

Many new inventions and improvements of earlier ones were introduced, but I can only attempt to refer to a few of these. Magazine rifles and pistols were invented on a new principle, as may be seen from examples in the Tower of London, Nos. 472 and 473, Class XII, which are fully described and illustrated in the Catalogue.

In the following chapter is fully described an Italian pistol of this type.

Revolving weapons showed marked improvement both in mechanism and workmanship, some examples being of the finest quality. These were made with two, three, four, six, and even seven barrels, a separate pan and steel in some cases being attached to each barrel, and, like the earlier examples, were revolved by hand.

In the Tower of London (Class XII, No. 47) may be seen a most interesting wheel-lock revolving carbine, described as early XVIIIth century. This has six chambers, and is revolved by hand. The lock of this is quite exceptional in having the doghead moving towards the muzzle (on the flint and snaphaunce principle). Further, this weapon proves the survival of the wheel-lock for some 200 years after its invention in 1517.

The desire to produce weapons capable of firing more than one charge from the same barrel still existed, and I shall attempt to describe a very interesting example in the following chapter.

The first invention of what might be termed a hammerless gun or pistol was introduced by Germany about the middle of the century. One of this type, fully described and illustrated in the Catalogue, may be seen in the Tower of London, No. 627, Class XII, the mark on the barrel being " STANISLAUS PACZELT 1738." The present writer until recently retained in his collection the pair of pistols shown in Fig. 84, of similar type, and by the same makers, but these were undated. The idea was ingenious, but the efficiency doubtful, and in all probability very few were made.

In the following chapter will be described and illustrated a few characteristic types and some examples of the rare and interesting weapons of this period.

CHAPTER VII

Examples of Early XVIIIth Century Firearms

DURING the first half of the XVIIIth century English gunsmiths began to compete keenly with those of the Continent, and before long were able to supply all the requirements of the country. It is, therefore, now possible to illustrate many characteristic examples of the various types of English weapons, and to compare these with the earlier and contemporary firearms produced by gunsmiths on the Continent.

Firstly, I will give a few illustrations of that rare and very interesting type having stocks and butts entirely of metal. The earliest examples were probably made at the commencement of the century, but their manufacture was continued until about the middle. Most of these were of the pocket type, but there are exceptions, as one of those pairs illustrated will show.

In Fig. 66 two interesting specimens are shown, the top one being a hand-revolved, four-barrel pistol, having a pan and steel to each barrel. By an upward pressure on the back part of the trigger guard, the catch retaining the barrels in position is released. This pistol bears the mark SEGALLAS—LONDON, and is 7½ inches long. The lower one is a good example of a two-barrel pistol of this type, having two dogheads, steels, and pans. This is marked M. MINIC, a maker whom I have been unable to trace. The stocks and butts of both are well engraved, as are all of this type.

Fig. 67 illustrates two early and interesting examples, the lower one, 5 inches long, having two barrels (under and over), with two side locks. This pistol, although not fitted with folding triggers, has no trigger guard, which, combined with the fact that the barrels are rifled, is worthy of note, being quite exceptional. The locks are marked NIQUET DE JEUNE (a Liège gunsmith of some repute). The one shown at the top (8 inches long) is also interesting, and of the finest workmanship. This is marked " London," but has no gunsmith's name.

In Fig. 68 a pair of single pistols by Cracknell, with London proof mark, are illustrated, their length being 7¼ inches. The barrels, as may be seen, are chiselled, each with a different design, and the stocks, deeply engraved, show traces of gilding.

In Fig. 69 a group of four pistols is shown, all being of this type. The small one at the bottom of the plate is a gunmaker's model, being only 3¾ inches long, but the lock and decorative finish are of the finest workmanship and design. Its case contains a key for screwing off the barrel, also a second and shorter barrel, which can alternately be fitted. The second from the top has a secret folding trigger and a safety bolt, and is marked SEGALAS—LONDON. The other two are by the same maker, and the length of these is about 6 inches.

Fig. 70 illustrates an exceptionally fine pair marked NICHOLSON, CORN-HILL, LONDON. These, for the type, are unusually long, being 12¼ inches, and of the finest workmanship and finish. The barrels bear the London proof mark and I.R.

In the following Fig., 71, are shown two metal-butted pistols.

The lower one is by Segallas, London, and has two barrels (side by side).

The other one is an interesting and probably unique alarm pistol, which, although unmarked, is undoubtedly of English origin.

By the fixing of this to a stake, after attaching a cord to the lever under the barrel, the pistol will fire on any strain being placed on the cord, on the same principle as an ordinary alarm gun.

I will now briefly describe, with the help of illustrations, the typical cannon-barrel pistol with wooden stock.

The pair illustrated in Fig. 72 are fine examples of the earliest form, the barrels (at the breech end) being octagonal, and the lock and barrel in one piece. They are 13 inches long, and marked on the lock plates CORNFORTI. The butt caps and furnishings are of steel, which is unusual in this type.

In the next Fig., 73, are shown right- and left-handed English pocket pistols. These are 7½ inches long, one being marked W. TURVEY, LONDON, and dated 1730.

Fig. 74 illustrates a fine pair of French pistols of early type, marked LEMAIRE, which are 11½ inches long, and have plain silver butt caps.

In the following Fig., 75, are shown another fine pair marked T. RICHARDS, being 12 inches long. These, like the preceding pairs, are of the earlier period.

In Fig. 76 is shown a fine and uncommon pair, marked DELANY LONDON. These have separate side locks, and the stock cut off square under the breech, which proves them to be of a rather later date. Their length is 12½ inches.

In the following Fig., 77, is given an example of a cannon-barrel pistol, with the swivel ring attachment to the barrel referred to in the previous chapter. This is marked I. DAFTE, and is 16¼ inches long.

The following are examples of pistols of the same type, but of a later period, having the doghead in the centre of the action, and the pan and steel placed on the top of the barrel.

In Fig. 78 is an exceptionally fine pair of double-barrel pistols, each barrel having a separate doghead, steel, and pan. These are marked KETLAND & Co., the length being 13¼ inches, which is quite unusual in this type. The next Fig., 79, illustrates one marked " K " (doubtless made by Ketland at rather a later date), the total length of which is 21 inches. This is probably an example of a pistol manufactured for export to a country where, in order to prevent the importation of pistols, firearms under a certain length were prohibited. After importation it was an easy matter to shorten the barrel to the ordinary pistol length.

The latest and most beautiful form of this type are those shown in Fig. 80. It will be seen that the stocks of these are of a different form, bulging sharply towards the butt, and that the silver wire and inlay work are of exceptionally fine quality.

Figs. 81 and 82 illustrate four very fine examples of double-barrel pistols of this type (being, with one exception, London made), all of the finest quality and workmanship. The top one in Fig. 81 is by AISLABIE— LONDON, and the other, marked TOCHARD ARQUEBUSIER DU ROY A PARIS, is a single-trigger pistol with a secret folding trigger. In Fig. 82, the top one is by Taylor, and the other by Tow, both London gunsmiths.

In Fig. 83 is shown a very fine example of an English hunting sword, having a pistol with cannon barrel attached, the lock being marked I. HARRIS. This has the original scabbard marked BECKETT, ST. JAMES. Both the sword and scabbard are beautifully mounted in silver, and the total length is 31½ inches. This, being English, is interesting, for the majority of those handed down to us were made on the Continent, where hunting swords with pistols attached were much in favour at this time.

In Fig. 84 is shown an example of an English seven-barrel revolving pistol (bearing the London proof mark) made by Hunter, probably towards the middle of the XVIIIth century. This is revolved by hand, the catch retaining the barrels in position being actuated by a spring, which, by means of a turnscrew, can either be strengthened or weakened. Two of the barrels, namely, the one immediately under the flash pan and the centre one, fire simultaneously when the bolt (affixed to the lock plate) is pushed in, after which the remaining five are fired separately. Probably after loading this bolt was pushed in, thus insuring a double discharge for the first shot. A common flash pan serves for all barrels, which, together with the turnscrew and bolt, may be seen in the illustration. The length of this is 9½ inches, and, although a somewhat clumsy weapon, is of good workmanship and ingenious mechanism. It is interesting as being, in all probability, England's first attempt to produce a seven-barrel revolving pistol.

The next Fig., 85, shows a very fine pair of holster pistols, 15 inches long, by BRANDER. MINORIES. LONDON (Brander was first established in London about 1637). These were formerly in the Author's collection, and are fine examples of pistols produced about the middle of the century, the workmanship of both the locks and silver furnishings being of the highest standard. These have barrels of gun metal, and trigger guards of silver.

In the following Figures are shown a few typical specimens of Italian firearms, which even at this time could not be surpassed, either for artistic merit or fine workmanship.

Fig. 86 illustrates an exceptionally fine pair of double-barrel (under and over) revolving pistols, having a separate pan and steel to each barrel. These, of unusual length, being 21½ inches, have furnishings of brass, well chiselled in the best style, and are good examples of the fine quality of the workmanship and artistic decoration of the Northern Italian gunsmith's work at this time. In the following Fig., 87, is shown another fine pair with graceful lines and artistic furnishings of brass, with silver medallions. Both barrels and locks are marked G. STORNATTI, and their length is 19 inches. These also are probably North Italian.

An interesting pair of pistols, having Southern Italian locks and Spanish barrels, with mounts and furnishings of brass, well engraved, are illustrated in Fig. 88, their length being 17½ inches. The butt caps are octagonal, and I am inclined to think that these were probably made in Italy for the Spanish market, and Spanish barrels fitted. The locks bear the mark F.M., and are of the finest quality of this period.

With the kind permission of Mr. W. H. Fenton I am able to illustrate in Fig. 89 a pair of Italian magazine pistols of the middle of the century.

The top of the butt cap covers the entrance to the magazine for bullets, and the plate opposite the lock contains the entrance to the magazine for powder. They also have separate magazines for priming, which are placed underneath the flash pan. These pistols will be seen to have a cylinder (which, by means of a lever, is revolved by hand) containing one receptacle just large enough to receive a bullet, and another of the size to receive one charge of powder.

In order to load, it is necessary to point the muzzle downwards, and at the same time revolve the cylinder, which action drops the bullet into the barrel and the powder behind it. The pan, by the same movement, is primed, and the pistol ready to fire.

These pistols have screw barrels enabling them, if desired, to be loaded in the usual manner.

In England both pistols and guns were made on this principle towards the end of the century, but in the English magazine firearms the entrances to the magazine, both for bullets and powder, were close together on the plate on the opposite side to the lock. The writer previously owned a pistol by Mortimer, London, made (on this system) at about the end of the century.

In Fig. 90 is given a typical example of a pair of German pistols of the period. These are marked JOSEPH HAUER, probably a descendant of Anton Hauer, who is said to have been established in Nuremberg in 1612. The mounts and furnishings are of metal, of fine quality, gilded and deeply engraved with battle scenes. The following Fig., 91, illustrates a typical pair of Dutch pistols (19 inches long), furnished and mounted in the best style in chiselled steel, having well-carved stocks and locks of fine workmanship marked THEODORUS COOP. UTRECHT. These are fine examples of Dutch pistols of this period.

Fig. 92 shows a double-barrel (under and over) sporting gun, dated 1720, by Languedon, Paris. This is 49 inches long, has a separate steel and pan to each barrel, and by an upward pressure on the fore part of the trigger guard, the barrels can be revolved by hand. It is interesting as a rare type of sporting gun of this period, and is well finished and mounted.

In Fig. 93 are illustrated two fine pistols, the top one being marked JOHANN. DEHLAN. A PRAG., the length of which is 18½ inches. This is beautifully mounted with silver medallions on brass, and has a finely chiselled barrel. The lower one is marked JOSEPH FRUEWERTH A. FORCHENSTAIN, being 19½ inches long, and mounted with silver furnishings in the best style. Although of a much earlier date, this pistol is said to have been presented by Napoleon to Marshal Lannes.

Fig. 94 illustrates the pair of hammerless pistols referred to in the last chapter.

In these, the doghead is actuated by, and attached to, a spiral spring, which is contained within the breech end of the barrel, and the face of the triangular wedge (shown in the illustration) forms the steel, immediately below which is placed the flash pan.

On pulling the trigger the spiral spring is released, causing the flint holder to strike the steel with sufficient force to fire the priming in the pan.

This invention may be described as more interesting than practical.

There are other firearms of this period which I would like to have mentioned, but space is limited. I can only hope, therefore, that those shown may convey some idea of the different styles of decoration, and various types of weapons, used in Europe at this time.

PLATE XXXVII

FIG. 66

PLATE XXXVIII

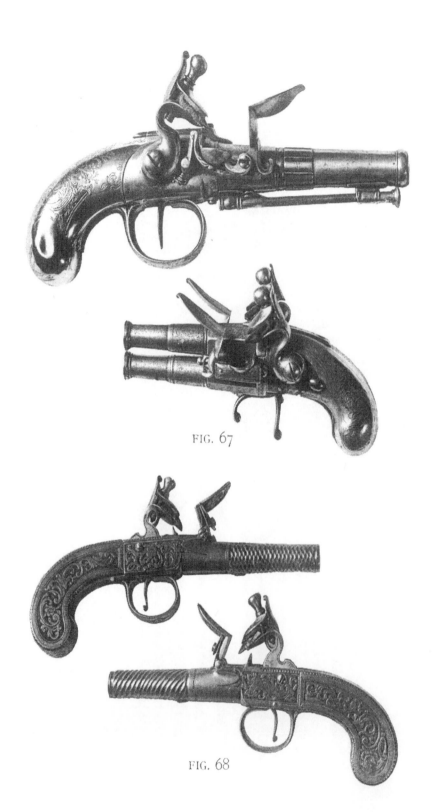

FIG. 67

FIG. 68

PLATE XXXIX

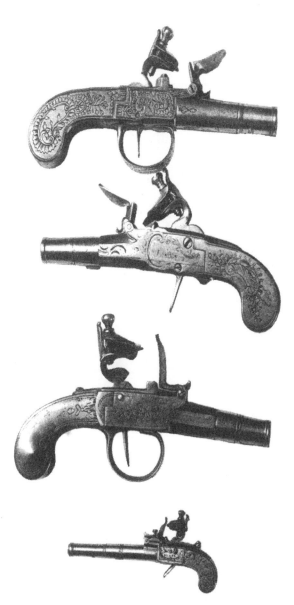

FIG. 69

PLATE XL

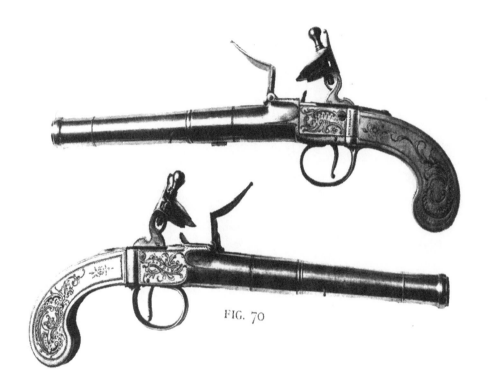

FIG. 70

PLATE XLI

FIG. 71

PLATE XLII

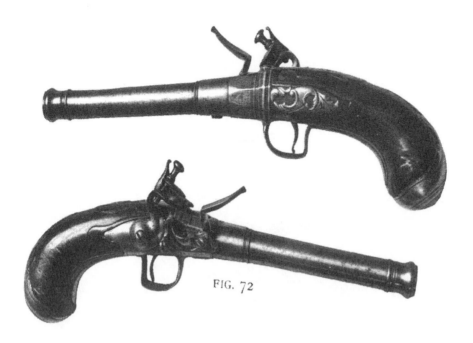

FIG. 72

FIG. 73

PLATE XLIII

FIG. 74

FIG. 75

PLATE XLIV

FIG. 76

FIG. 77

PLATE XLV

FIG. 78

PLATE XLVI

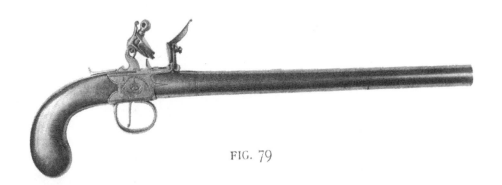

FIG. 79

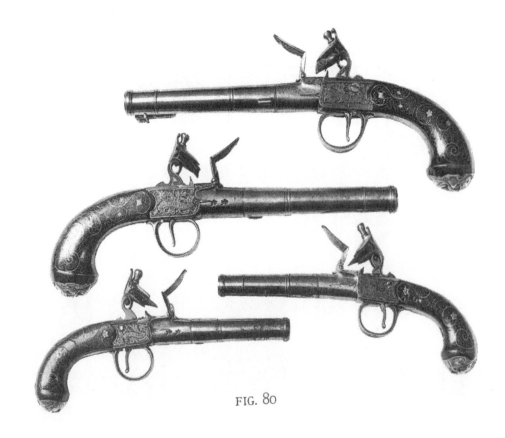

FIG. 80

PLATE XLVII

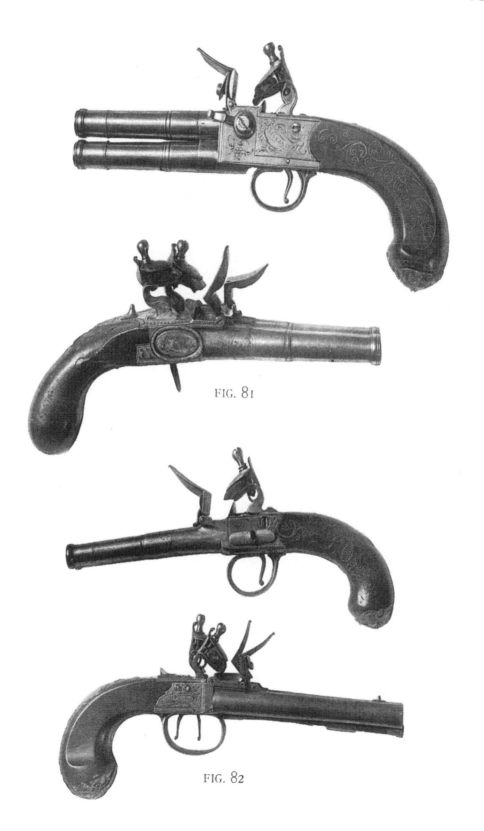

FIG. 81

FIG. 82

PLATE XLVIII

FIG. 83

FIG. 84

PLATE XLIX

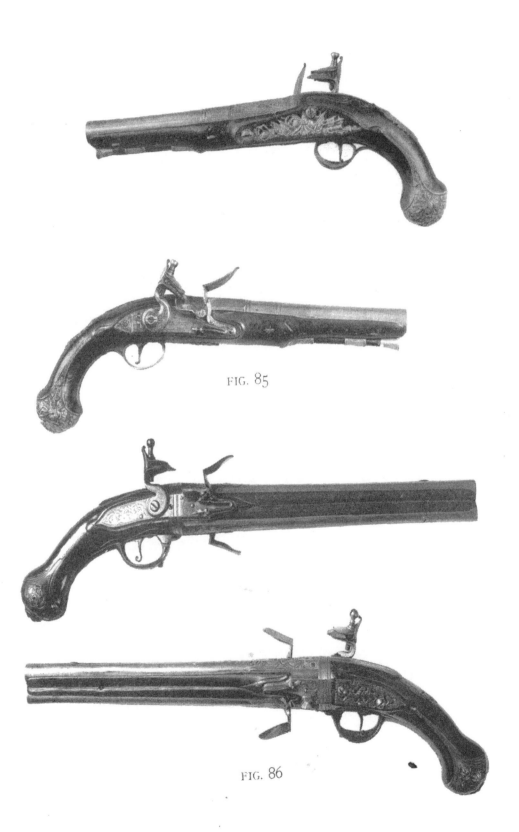

FIG. 85

FIG. 86

PLATE L

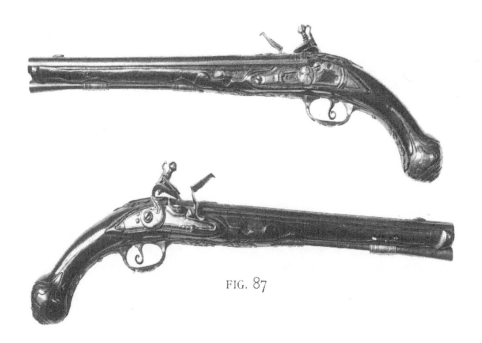

FIG. 87

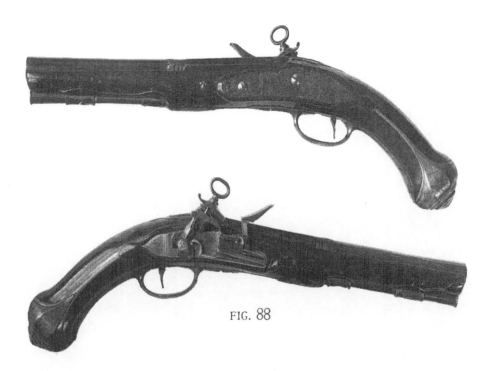

FIG. 88

PLATE LI

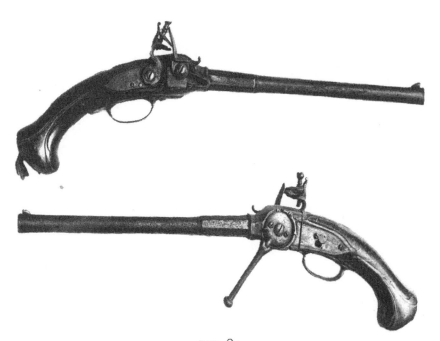

FIG. 89

PLATE LII

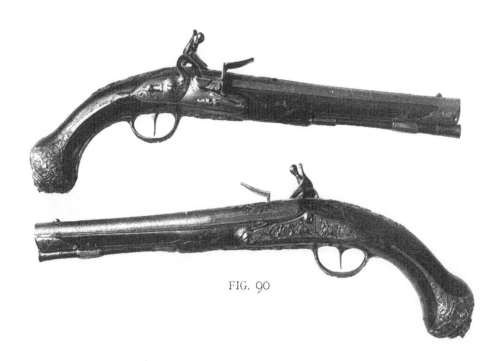

FIG. 90

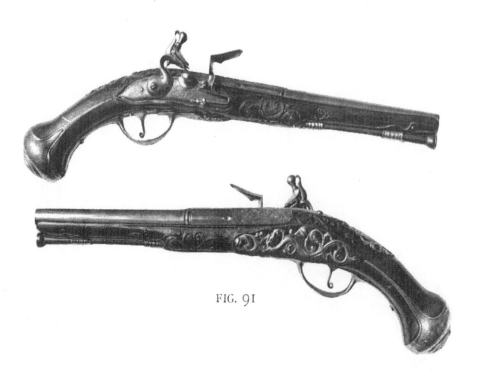

FIG. 91

PLATE LIII

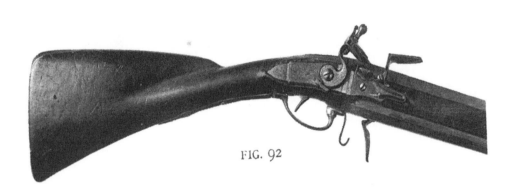

FIG. 92

Town, Butcher coll.

PLATE LIV

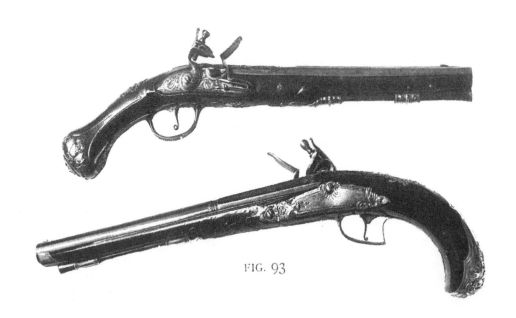

FIG. 93

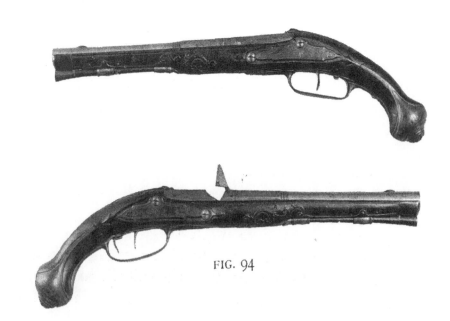

FIG. 94

CHAPTER VIII

FIREARMS IN THE LATTER PART OF THE XVIIITH CENTURY

S the century advanced there was a further marked falling off in the true artistic merit and beauty of design of the mounts and furnishings, but, on the other hand, a rapid advance was made both in the efficiency and fine workmanship of the firearms produced. In most cases, decorative furnishings and mounts were entirely dispensed with, or otherwise replaced by those of a plain and simple form.

Gunsmiths began to realize that "fine feathers" by no means always make "fine birds," and that artistic and elaborate furnishings, although considerably increasing the cost of production, neither added to the efficiency nor shooting quality of the weapon. They, therefore, ignored the question of art, and concentrated their energy on producing weapons of precision and efficiency, combined with fine workmanship and finish. By so doing they were able to reduce the cost, and to bring these within the reach of the many instead of the few.

There is, however, an exception, for it is generally agreed that Scottish pistols produced about the middle of this century, and for some time afterwards, were more perfect in type, artistic design, and finish than at any previous period.

New ideas continued to be recorded, but no invention of prime importance was made, with the possible exception of the breech-loading rifle in 1776 by Captain Fergusson.

Many of the inventions were ingenious, but the majority proved of little practical value. For instance, in 1799 Edward Thomason invented a mechanism which caused the flint holder automatically to present a slightly different angle to the steel at each discharge, the idea being to insure better

37

sparking. By others, the same result was obtained by the turn of a screw affixed to the side of the flint holder.

The blunderbus, although invented at a much earlier date, was probably now in greater favour than at any previous period, and especially in this country. Many had folding spring bayonets attached either under, at the side of, or over the barrel, the point being held either by a sliding trigger guard or a spring bolt. The bayonets, when released (by pulling back the trigger guard or bolt), were forced into position by a spring, and held there by a catch.

Although not firearms, I think it should be mentioned that during this century much study and thought were given to the development and improvement of the air gun and pistol, very many of which were manufactured.

The air gun was probably invented about the middle of the XVIIth century, and the following extract from the Addendum to " English Military Discipline," published in 1680, is interesting :

> I saw in a Gentleman's house of Picardy near St. Quentin, an Arquebusse or Wind Gun that was charged with the Wind, whose bullet at thirty paces distance pierced a door two inches thick.

It is also said to have been adopted during the Austrian War for military purposes, and to have been used by certain regiments as their special weapon. As an example of the later type, I give, in Fig. 95, a fine specimen of an English air pistol, marked JOSEPH DAVIDSON, BOROUGH, LONDON. This has a brass barrel and silver furnishings (the hall-mark on the latter being 1796), and a skeleton stock which can be attached.

It is only possible to give a short description of some of the more interesting and typical weapons of this period, most of which are English.

During the second half of the XVIIIth century the gunsmiths of this country obtained a world-wide reputation, the result being that they made many of the more interesting and typical weapons used in the various quarters of the globe.

With the kind permission of Messrs. Lloyd and Son I am able to illustrate, in Fig. 96, a remarkable and probably unique pistol. This pistol fires four separate charges from one barrel, the charges being rammed one on the top of the other. The four locks (two on each side of the barrel) are so placed that their flash pans exactly correspond with the touch holes, bored equidistant along the barrel, and the four triggers are ingeniously arranged. With this weapon the greatest accuracy in loading must have been necessary to insure that each charge exactly corresponded with the touch holes. Great care also was imperative when firing, for the top charge in the barrel had to be fired first, and the others in rotation. As there are four triggers, the mistake of pulling the wrong one could very easily be made, the result of which would prove disastrous. This pistol bears no maker's name, but is undoubtedly English, and probably made for boarding purposes. Although a somewhat clumsy weapon, the mechanism is both interesting and ingenious.

Fig. 97 illustrates an exceptionally fine specimen of a double-barrel, single-trigger, pocket pistol, by that well-known gunsmith Joseph Egg, the hall-marks on the mounts of which show its date to be 1785. It is but 6 inches long, and a good example of the high standard of workmanship and finish attained by English gunsmiths of this period. The locks are fitted with safety bolts, and a spring bayonet is attached to the barrel. The trigger guard and butt are of silver, well engraved, and the butt cap and escutcheon of gold.

In Fig. 98 are shown two typical examples of bell-mouthed pistols with bayonets attached. The top one (14 inches long) is marked WATERS & Co., and represents the type of blunderbus pistol usually carried on stage coaches. The lower one (9 inches long) is marked W. BOND, 59, LOMBARD STREET, LONDON, and is more of the boarding type. In the next Fig., 99, are illustrated two other pistols with bayonets attached (both 8½ inches long); the upper one, having two barrels (under and over), is by NICHOLSON, LONDON, and the lower one (with three barrels) by HEWSON, EXETER.

It will be of interest to illustrate in Fig. 100 a double-barrel English sporting gun by Tow, LONDON, who was established about the middle of the century. This represents the best type of a sporting gun of this period, and the balance, graceful lines, and workmanship could not be surpassed. It further proves the great advance made by leading English gunsmiths towards the attainment of perfect workmanship and efficiency.

Fig. 101 illustrates what may be considered a typical pair of pistols of the best military type of the XVIIIth century, marked STANTON, LONDON, their length being 13¾ inches. These have steel butts and trigger guards, with silver escutcheons, and are good examples of fine workmanship and finish.

In the next Fig., 102, are two interesting types of pistols with four barrels. The top one, 11½ inches long, is marked J. PROBIN, and fires the four barrels simultaneously. The lower one, marked D. EGG, LONDON, is 9½ inches long, the barrels of which are fired separately by means of a sliding pan cover and revolving touch holes. Fig. 103 illustrates a well made and finished pair of double-barrel (under and over) pistols, 8 inches long, by TAYLOR & CO. LONDON, each barrel being fired separately by means of a revolving touch hole. The stocks of these are inlaid with silver wirework, and have silver escutcheons.

In the next Fig., 104, is shown the interior view of an English lock, which is quite exceptional, having no screws in any part of it, the whole mechanism being held in place by a detachable plate.

Fig. 105 illustrates the lock (already mentioned) having a screw affixed to the side of the cock, the turning of which alters the angle presented by the flint to the steel. This is marked G. BOLTON ESQR. LONDINI. INVT. PATENT T. FISHER, MAKER. In Fig. 106 are shown a pair of fine quality duelling pistols, by Joseph Manton, which are typical of those made during the last years of this century.

In Fig. 107 is shown a late type of Spanish pistol, dated 1810, from which it may be noted how little Spanish pistols of the early XIXth century varied from those of the earlier types.

Many other examples might be given, but those illustrated show most of the different types in favour at this period.

PLATE LV

FIG. 95

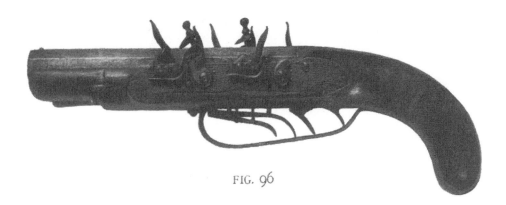

FIG. 96

PLATE LVI

FIG. 97

PLATE LVII

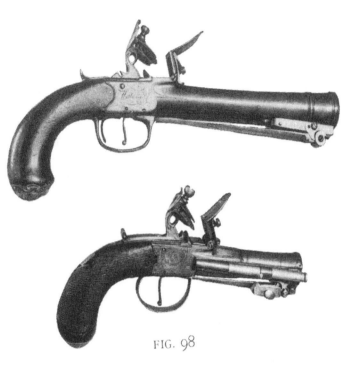

FIG. 98

FIG. 99

PLATE LVIII

FIG. 100

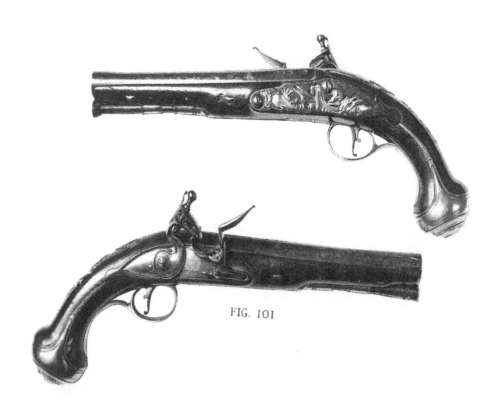

FIG. 101

PLATE LIX

FIG. 102

FIG. 103

PLATE LX

FIG. 104

FIG. 105

PLATE LXI

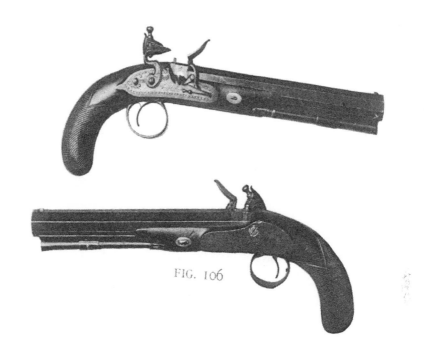

FIG. 106

FIG. 107

CHAPTER IX

THE PERIOD OF TRANSITION FROM THE FLINT TO THE PERCUSSION SYSTEM

BEFORE concluding, I feel compelled to treat briefly of this interesting transition, and to attempt to prove that in other countries the detonating system was applied to small arms quite early in the XVIIIth century.

In England the first patent was granted to the Reverend Alexander John Forsyth in 1807, in the specifications for which he fully described his system of detonation and the various means in which it could be applied to small arms and cannon.

Subsequently, however, the validity of his patent was disputed, it being contended that a similar invention had previously been made and adopted by certain gunsmiths in Europe. It would be interesting to know what evidence at the eventual trial was adduced in support of this claim, and to learn whether the Spanish invention, which I am about to describe, was then mentioned.

The fact that Forsyth was able to establish his patent for this country proves that no similar invention had previously been used here. Therefore, so far as we are concerned, it is impossible to give too high an appreciation of Forsyth's invention, which certainly originated our percussion system.

In Fig. 108 is illustrated a finely chiselled and well-finished lock, firing on a detonating principle, and detached from a Spanish sporting gun. This is inscribed Jh. GUTIERREZ SEVILLA 1720, and on the barrel is a lion rampant. Dates on firearms are always open to suspicion (many having been added at a later period). In this case, however, it may be judged to be correct, not only from the type of the lock and quality and style of the chiselling, but also from the type of the weapon itself.

Auguste Demmin, in "Arms and Armour," includes in his list of Spanish armourers Anton Gutierrez, but gives neither date nor the town in which he worked. Probably Joseph Gutierrez was one of his descendants, in which case Anton doubtless also worked at Seville, where many fine arms were produced.

I have been unable to discover any other firearms of so early a date fired on this principle, and must, therefore, conclude that the invention originated in Spain.

The striker, in the form of a dog, is attached by a connecting rod to the magazine, the top of which represents a rabbit squatting, the chiselling of the whole lock being of the finest quality and in the best Spanish style. When at full cock the magazine, containing detonating powder, is held exactly above the touch hole, and, on pulling the trigger, the magazine slides back, leaving in the small pan sufficient detonating powder to be fired by the striker. The screw seen in the middle of this lock is a hollow one, forming the touch hole, and was doubtless made with the idea that, being detachable, it could be more easily cleaned and freed from fouling.

Although revolutionizing the previously accepted theory, I fear, in face of the convincing evidence of this Spanish gun, we can no longer claim for Forsyth the original invention of applying the detonating system to small arms, but only the introduction to this country of a similar invention in a more advanced form.

In Fig. 109 is shown a magazine primer as designed by Forsyth for small arms. This was screwed in to the side of the barrel, and in order to deposit sufficient detonating powder in the cavity lying immediately below the plunger, had to be revolved and then brought back to its original position.

Very shortly after this detonating pellets were used in place of powder, and on the same plate may be seen a priming flask, so designed that by slowly revolving the disc one pellet at a time can be dropped. The interior view of the detached disc is also illustrated in order to show the cavities round the rim, which each hold one pellet. The remaining two pieces shown on this plate are different systems for the converting of flint-lock weapons to percussion.

The next Fig., 110, illustrates a most interesting lock (being a combination of flint and percussion) made by that celebrated gun maker, Ezekiel Baker. This lock, by means of a sliding block, can effectively and alternately be used for either system, and is a good example of ingenious mechanism and workmanship. It is inscribed E. BAKER 1821, and is the most practical combination lock I have seen of this period. In 1822 a somewhat similar combination lock was patented by Samson Davis.

In the year 1818 Joseph Manton patented a small hollow tube, made of thin metal filled with detonating powder, and also a special form of lock to be used with this. The latter is illustrated in Fig. 111, and was known as the tube lock.

The copper cap is supposed to have been invented in America about 1816, but was not used in this country until about 1820.

PLATE LXII

FIG. 108

FIG. 109

PLATE LXIII

FIG. 110

FIG. 111

CHAPTER X

SOME HINTS ON THE CLEANING AND KEEPING OF FIREARMS

HE remarks in this chapter are written with the hope that they may prove helpful to the uninitiated, and those who have but recently acquired the hobby for collecting. They may also possibly find some interest with those who, in the past, have been content to leave their cleaning and restoration to professionals.

I am convinced that, provided a collector has sufficient knowledge, and is prepared to devote the necessary time and trouble to the process, he cannot fail to obtain the best results. The professional cleaner is naturally unable to afford the time, and is consequently forced to shorten the process by using more drastic measures. It is further unreasonable to expect that he can take the same interest in the result as the collector who possesses any love for his hobby. How often do we come across what can only be described as highly burnished wrecks of really fine examples; the original surface, together with the crispness and beauty of the engraving or chiselling, having disappeared. This, too often, is the result of what is known as " over-cleaning," which, in other words, is cleaning by too drastic a method. The softest and finest quality of buffing-brush may be used as a finishing touch only, but otherwise avoid a lathe and stick to your hands and the result will repay. The old adage, " experientia docet," is as true to-day as it ever was, and is peculiarly applicable in this case.

In the course of collecting, many specimens will be met with in a very rusted and bad condition, making it somewhat difficult to judge of their merit. It should, however, be possible to decide from the type and style of the weapon not only the approximate date, but also the country of origin. Before buying weapons in this condition a careful examination is necessary, in the first place, to ascertain that no parts of the lock or mounts are missing, and secondly, to see that the furnishings are of the style which should be found on this type, and that the stock, if damaged, is not beyond repair. Being satisfied on these points, the worst grade of condition would not stop my acquiring the weapon, for it is preferable to buy them in this state than "over cleaned." Naturally, knowledge and experience lessens speculation, but there are few experts who have not bought their experience, and fewer who regret this. The collector who has never made a mistake is, indeed, a "rara avis," but on the other hand there are probably few who in the course of years have not obtained some pieces which, after careful cleaning, have revealed treasures in art beyond their highest hopes. In the following remarks, I must presume the collector is possessed of the few necessary tools, namely:

Small parallel vice.
A small cramp (for taking off the mainspring).
Pair of flat-nosed pliers.
Pair of round-nosed pliers.
Pair of parallel pliers.
An assortment of finest small files.
A few fine wire brushes.
An assortment of screwdrivers.
Two small punches.

A good stock of the finest grades of emery cloth, and also some fine emery powder should be kept.

After having secured the weapon, the first thing to be done is to take it to pieces. It is advisable to commence operations by driving out, with a small punch, the pin bolts holding the barrel, and also those holding the pipes (ramrod holders), and then to draw out the screw which, passing through the tang of the breech plug, secures the barrel. Before, however, taking the barrel off, it is advisable to withdraw the screws holding the lock, which will also release the escutcheon on the opposite side. After taking these off, remove the barrel. Then comes the trigger guard, which can usually be detached by withdrawing the pin holding the fore part. When the lock is off this pin can be seen, and the other end of the guard will be found to be either screwed or clipped in. This only leaves the butt and back escutcheon, which in many cases are difficult to remove, but these can be treated and cleaned where they are. Before proceeding further, I would advise placing all these pins, screws, and pieces together in a box, or they may easily get lost. Something definite may now be seen as to the condition of the stock, and if, as often is the case, the fore part carrying the barrel is either cracked or weakened by age, this must be strengthened. A broad piece of tape glued on the inside will usually suffice, but care must be taken that this does not overlap the edge. When thoroughly dry, carefully rub the whole of the stock with paraffin, using a soft piece of flannel, and continue doing this until all dirt and stains are removed. The metal butt and back escutcheon should at the same time be well rubbed with paraffin. After this, give the whole of the stock (but not the butt and escutcheon) a good dressing with refined linseed oil, rubbing this well in, and after a few hours repeat the operation. Several dressings at intervals of twenty-four hours are advisable, and what remains may be rubbed off, and a good polish obtained with a leather. We now come to the barrel, lock, and furnishings, which, in this case, are presumed to be in a very rusted and bad condition, but showing faintly some traces of engraving and chiselling. Place all these together in a vessel of some sort with sufficient paraffin to cover them, and leave them to soak for from two days to a week, according to condition. The butt and back escutcheon, unless removed, cannot be treated in this way, and therefore must be liberally dabbed with paraffin at frequent intervals, and, if possible, not allowed to become dry. They should, in fact, be dabbed with paraffin every few hours for some days. After this pickling process, take all the pieces out and rub them hard with soft flannel, when it will be found that a good deal of rust will come away, then well and carefully brush them all over with a fine wire brush and replace in the paraffin, repeating this operation at intervals of a day or two, until able to see well-defined traces of the original surface, engraving, or chiselling, as the case may be. When this stage is reached, and whilst wet with paraffin, sprinkle a little fine emery powder over the surface, and brush briskly with a fine wire brush. This, in most cases, gives the desired result without wearing away the crispness or beauty of the engraving and chiselling. The finishing touch may then be given, first, by rubbing lightly with the finest grade of emery cloth, and afterwards with a wire brush. In many cases it will be found that the rust has but very slightly affected the original surface, and very often what appeared to be hopeless rust proves to be a mixture of rust, dirt, and oil. If the attempt were made to remove this without the pickling process, it may now be judged what drastic measures would be required, and what the subsequent result must be.

I have purposely left the question of the lock until the last, for it is most necessary that before taking this entirely to pieces it should be well pickled in order that the small screws of the mechanism may the more easily be extracted. In the first place, take off the mainspring, before doing which, full cock the lock and well cramp the spring with the small cramp mentioned. The spring can then be withdrawn from the plate, after taking out the pin or screw which holds it. In cases of very strong springs, the vice may be found necessary. Having accomplished this, it will be found easy to take the remainder of the mechanism to pieces, and to detach the doghead and steel from the lock plate, after which it is advisable to place all the screws and parts together in a box. The lock plate, flint holder, steel, springs, and every part of the mechanism must now be carefully cleaned (by the method already described), and, after oiling, replaced. It should then be found that the lock works smoothly and well. It may be remarked that when a screw or bolt is rusted in, force is useless until it has been thoroughly treated with paraffin. This can be done by depositing with a feather a few drops round the head of the screw, giving it time to soak down, also in the same way a few drops may with advantage be applied to the other end. Should it then refuse to move, place a punch on the top, giving a sharp tap or two with a hammer, and try again.

When using emery cloth, only use the finer grades, and sharp angles should be cleaned by wrapping this round a narrow and flat piece of wood. If it be desired to obtain a burnished surface, metal polish may be applied, which, when dry, should be brushed off with the finest wire brush, and the surface afterwards polished with a leather.

This, by many, may be considered a long and tedious process, but, nevertheless, will amply repay those who are willing to give the time and take the trouble.

Others may adopt different methods, but I doubt whether, in such cases, the same result can be obtained, either in a shorter time, or with less trouble. It must be remembered that the more thorough the cleaning, the less chance there is of rust, and pieces which have once been thoroughly cleaned, and afterwards oiled, should never require the same operation a second time.

Another method recommended for cleaning gun-locks (which, however, I have not tested) is as follows:

Place the lock in a vessel of water with a handful of ordinary washing soda and boil for an hour or more.

This dissolves the coagulated oil and loosens the rust, making it more easy to remove. It is necessary, however, that all springs should be detached, as otherwise they would snap by expansion.

In the event of this method being adopted, I would suggest the advisability of afterwards soaking in paraffin before attempting to remove the rust.

We now come to the important question as to how best to keep firearms in good condition. As far as the stocks are concerned, there is no better dressing than refined linseed oil. This should be applied either with a soft piece of rag, or flannel, and rubbed well in, but care must be taken to prevent, as far as is possible, the barrel and metal furnishings from becoming smeared with this. As regards the barrel, lock, and furnishings, all that is necessary is to rub them over from time to time with a few drops of the finest thin mineral oil.

It is certainly advisable to keep in glass-covered cases (made as damp and dust proof as possible) all the most valuable and finest weapons. This, however, is not possible with many guns and larger weapons, and as regards these, more care is, therefore, necessary. The metal parts should be well rubbed over with mineral oil, and the stocks with linseed oil, every few months, and naturally damp rooms and walls should be avoided.

H

A TREATISE ON SCOTTISH
HAND FIREARMS OF THE
XVITH, XVIITH & XVIIITH CENTURIES
BY C. E. WHITELAW, FELLOW
OF THE GLASGOW INSTITUTE OF ARCHITECTS AND
OF THE SOCIETY OF ANTIQUARIES OF SCOTLAND

PREFACE

THESE notes are the outcome of a careful study of Scottish Arms and Weapons carried on while gathering together a small representative collection of these, and of kindred objects which illustrate the development of Art and Craftsmanship in Scotland from Mediaeval times down to about 1850. This work has occupied much of my spare time over a period of some thirty years.

During the last two years I have examined a considerable body of documentary evidence bearing on Scottish Arms—a field of inquiry which has scarcely yet been touched—with which I am hoping to be able soon to deal.

In these notes space has not permitted more than a mere outline and summary of the subject of Scottish Firearms. I have, however, attempted to formulate a system of classification by which the distinctive types have been defined and the evolution of these types and of the lock mechanism made clear. This has not been done previously except by myself when arranging the exhibits and drawing up the introductory notes and catalogue entries for the Scottish Arms shown at the National Exhibition held in Edinburgh in 1908, and in Glasgow in 1911.

Types have been classified according to the form of the butt, while the chronological arrangement has been made to follow the evolution of the lock mechanism. For reasons stated later on no other system seems to be practicable.

C. E. W.

The Glasgow Literary Club,
Glasgow.
December, 1922.

CONTENTS

SCOTTISH FIREARMS

EVOLUTION AND CLASSIFICATION

INTRODUCTORY

IN Scotland, a country whose independence for centuries was only maintained by force of arms, and whose internal history down to the middle of the XVIIIth century was a record of civil wars and family feuds, the possession of arms was a necessity and not a luxury.

The production of native iron was very small in Scotland previous to the latter half of the XVIIIth century, therefore arms, or material for making them, had to be imported.

Judging by armourers' signatures and guild marks the imported weapons seem to have come mostly from Germany and the Low Countries, and probably a few from Spain. The iron was imported from England and Sweden, and from this a large quantity of arms was made in Scotland, where distinctly national types were developed. These arms are of particular interest, as the Celtic forms of decoration, which had died out in Europe by mediaeval times, survived in Scotland to a very late period, and were revived and applied in combination with contemporary ornament to the arms, accoutrements, and accessories of dress of the XVIIth and XVIIIth centuries.

The most interesting are the firearms which are shown by the records of the burghs and the Hammerman Craft to have been manufactured, as early as the XVIth century, in the principal towns of Scotland situated for the most part along or near to the eastern seaboard, from whence development would naturally spread to the clan armourers of the central and western Highlands. The characteristics of these weapons suggest that they were evolved from the Dutch pieces imported into the country during the XVIth century.

I

General Remarks

In fixing dates for Scottish types it must be borne in mind that the limits assigned to each period must be considered as elastic, there always being a considerable overlap through quicker development taking place nearer to the sources of advancement and spreading gradually to more remote parts. Therefore, in dating pieces any period can only be approximate in a wide sense. The snaphaunce is the earliest form of native-made firearm identifiable,[1] and can be put as from the XVIth century to about 1675. Approximately the flint-lock dates from 1675 to 1820, and the percussion lock from 1820 to 1850.

The following article describes in detail the development in Scotland of guns and pistols, commencing with the former.

The Musket and Arquebus

The guns are remarkable for grace of form and decoration, varying in length from 3 ft. 10 in. to 6 ft. 10 in., the shorter being the arquebus or hagbut, the longer the musket (fired from a rest).[2] In the finest examples the barrels are ornamented by moulded cross bands or longitudinal fluting, and inlaid with silver. The stocks have thin narrow butts taking a graceful curve, fluted and elaborately carved with delicate running leaf scroll and grotesque animal forms (Plates I and II). The metal mounts are of silver or brass, and delicately engraved with designs such as rosettes and running leaf scrolls.

The trigger is of lobe shape or fitted with a ball terminal of silver or brass, but, except in the very earliest specimens, there is no trigger guard.

The locks are good in design and workmanship, and finely engraved, but as they are similar to those of the pistols, they will be dealt with together. Of the thirteen guns preserved in Castle Grant three are rifles, one (Plate I, Fig. 4) being also a breechloader.

The total number of Scottish guns still in existence in this country, so far as ascertained up to date, is twenty-one.[3]

The national type evidently died out shortly before the close of the

XVIIth century, when the flint-lock brought in the stock of the universal conventional pattern.

The earliest gun which has come under the notice of the writer is dated 1599. It is a wall-piece with fluted stock and steel mounts. The barrel is octagonal, with a moulded muzzle, terminating in a square block; the breech has a high comb with a peep-sight of three small perforations. There are three chiselled panels situated at intervals along the barrel: that at the breech has the pot of lilies, which is the insignia of the town of Dundee, and the date 1599; the central panel has the arms of the Campbells of Breadalbane; and the third panel encloses the initials (S.D.C.) of Sir Duncan Campbell. The present snaphaunce lock is plain, unsigned, and dated 1640. It has been taken from another piece.[4] The total length of this gun is 6 ft. 10 in., and its bore is $\frac{13}{16}$ in. (see page 61, Fig. A). This piece is fitted with a trigger guard.

THE PISTOL

Unlike the survivors of the Scottish type of gun in its national form, which cover the short period of about a hundred years, the pistol furnishes a complete sequence extending over a period of fully two hundred and fifty years—from late XVIth century down to about 1850. It shows a great variety in form, material, and decoration.

Scottish firearms may be divided into two classes according to lock mechanism.

Class I. The early snaphaunce.
The late snaphaunce.
II. The flint-lock.

CLASS I

The Early Snaphaunce

The known dated specimens of this class cover a period from 1598 to 1686.

The earliest pistols resolve themselves into two types—A and B.

Type A. Pistols of this type have a thin flat butt of a fish-tail form, terminating in a scroll-like outline resembling those found on German wheel-lock pistols of the early XVIth century. The stock may be of wood or metal: when of wood, it is mounted with brass or silver (Plate III, Figs. 9 and 11); when of metal, it is of brass (Plate III, Fig. 8). The writer has not found any of this type stocked in steel. The barrels and lock plates may be either of brass or steel.[5]

Type B. Pistols of this type have globose butts, after the fashion of contemporary foreign wheel-lock pistols. When the stock is of wood the butt may be of metal (Plate IV, Figs. 12 and 15); the stocks are, however, with few exceptions, of brass—rarely of steel [6]—and the butts, which vary in form, are sometimes pierced (Plate IV, Figs. 13 and 14).

In the earliest examples the barrels are usually of brass, ornamented with raised moulded cross bands, and engraving. The bore is small, slightly over $\frac{3}{8}$ in. (Plate IV, Fig. 13).

In general, the steel parts are blued and the locks engraved. The brass portions—stock, barrel, lock plate, and mounts—are engraved and sometimes gilt. The engraving is deeply cut, consisting mostly of running leaf scrolls, leaf ornament of other description, or conventional forms such as the fish scale. The rosette is the commonest flower form employed, but the thistle is also found. The ramrods are of steel, moulded at the extremities, but if the stock is of wood the ramrod is, in most cases, of wood also, tipped with bone or brass.

There is no trigger guard, and the extremity of the butt is usually fitted

THREE PANELS
ROUND MUZZLE
(HALF FULL SIZE)

FIG. **A.** RUBBINGS OF CHISELLED PANELS ON BARREL OF MUSKET DATED 1599.
(HALF FULL SIZE)
THE PROPERTY OF A.W.COX ESQ?

MAKERS STAMP
STRUCK ON THREE
INSET BRASS
ESCUTCHEONS AT BREECH
(FULL SIZE)

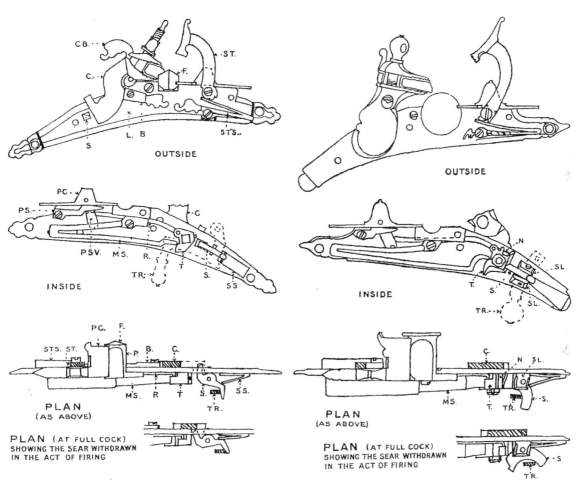

FIG. **B.** EARLY SNAPHAUNCE LOCK
(HALF FULL SIZE)

FIG. **C** LATE SNAPHAUNCE LOCK
(HALF FULL SIZE)

B.	BUFFER	**P.**	PAN	**SS.** SEAR SPRING
C.	COCK*	**PC.**	PAN-COVER.	**ST.** STEEL†
CB.	COMB	**PS.**	PAN-COVER SPRING	**STS.** STEEL SPRING
F.	FENCE	**PSV.**	PAN-COVER SWIVEL	**T.** TUMBLER
L.	LOCK-PLATE	**R.**	ROD CONNECTED TO TUMBLER	**TR.** TRIGGER
MS.	MAIN SPRING	**S.**	SEAR (OR SCEAR)	
N.	NOTCH IN TUMBLER TO RECEIVE THE SEAR	**SL.**	SEAR LUG	

* THIS PART IS SOMETIMES CALLED THE "DOGHEAD"

† THE CORRECT NAME FOR THIS PART IS THE "HAMMER." BUT AS THIS TERM WAS APPLIED, LATER, TO THE COCK OF PERCUSSION AND EARLY BREECH LOADING FIREARMS. "STEEL," WHICH WAS ALSO USED IN EARLY TIMES, HAS TO PREVENT CONFUSION, BEEN ADOPTED.

DIAGRAMS OF THE SNAPHAUNCE LOCK

with a steel picker to clear the touch hole, the head of the picker being, as a rule, perforated to hold a short lanyard.[7] In many of the later examples the trigger terminal is globular instead of lobe shaped. These pistols were made in pairs with right- and left-hand locks, and all are fitted with steel belt hooks. At this time the maker was designated a " Dagmaker," and merely punched his initials on the lock-plate. The date of manufacture was engraved across the breech of the barrel and, in most cases, on the fence of the lock also.

In the later examples (Plate III, Fig. 9, and Plate IV, Fig. 15) we find the barrels of steel, with the muzzle octagonal and slightly bell-mouthed, and the bore increased to $\frac{1}{2}$ in., a change introduced early in the second quarter of the XVIIth century. In this case the system of decoration is altered to meet the change of material. Engraving on blued steel would give a very small return for the labour entailed ; therefore, the raised bands were either left plain, or plated by a broad inset belt of silver or brass, on which the engraver exercised his art. The stocks were left plain or decorated only with a couple of small panels on the butt.

In common with all early types, the butts of the Scottish pistols of Class I have only a slight curve downwards from the stock.

Mechanism of the Early Snaphaunce Lock. (Class I)

The earliest form of lock (page 61, Fig. B) consists of the lock plate (L), to which are attached, externally, the pan (P), with a fence (F); over the pan is a sliding pan-cover (PC), above this the steel (ST). The cock (C) holds the pyrite or flint between the two jaws, which are closed by a pin held at the underside of the lower jaw by a small driving pin, and tightened by a nut screwed down over the upper jaw. When at full cock (there is no half cock) the cock is held by the nose of the sear (S), which projects through a square aperture in the lock plate and grips over the spur at the base, and to the rear, of the cock. On pressing the trigger (TR) the nose of the sear is withdrawn, and the cock falls, striking the pyrite or flint against the steel, and thereby generating the spark that ignites the powder in the pan. In falling, the cock pushes back the pan cover by means of a small rod (R) inside the lock, and connected to the tumbler (T), thus exposing the priming to the sparks. The fall of the cock is received on a buffer (B). Other parts of the lock are: steel spring (STS), pan cover spring (PS), pan cover swivel (PSV), main spring (MS), sear spring (SS), sear lug (SL).

The later examples of this form have the pin and nut of the cock combined into a pin, screwed through the lower jaw, as in the ordinary flint-lock (Plate I, Fig. 4). The fence of the earliest examples is small and hexagonal (Plate III, Fig. 11), while in the later it is large and circular (Plate I, Fig. 4).

In the latest specimens the body of the cock is widened so as to absorb the spur, a square aperture being cut in it to receive the nose of the sear.

In the metal-stocked pistols the trigger is hung on a pin screwed through the stock, above the lock plate. In the wooden-stocked pistols and guns a driving-pin is used.

There are two weak points in these locks (which they have in common with foreign firearms of the same type and period), there is, first, no bridle to hold together the interior mechanism, although several have a bridle on the steel, and, second, they have no provision for half cock. As Scottish pistols have no trigger guard or safety catch, it must have been difficult with safety to carry them loaded and primed.

THE LATE SNAPHAUNCE

The known dated specimens of this class cover the period from 1647 to 1702. During this stage the two most characteristically Scottish types were evolved. The great majority of examples which survive to the present day belong to the period from the end of the XVIIth to the end of the XVIIIth century. These survivors consist, with few exceptions, of the finest specimens because they were kept by old Highland families for use as accessories of the ceremonial Highland dress.

Type C. From the globose butt (Plate IV, Fig. 13) evolved the heart-shaped butt (Plate V, Fig. 17).

Pistols of this type were made in the districts bordering on the east coast, and may, therefore, be looked upon as a Lowland type. They appear to have gone out of fashion, and to have been replaced about the middle of the XVIIIth century by pistols with wooden stocks of the general conventional pattern.

Type D. From the fish-tail butt (Plate III, Fig. 9) evolved the scroll butt (Plate III, Fig. 10).

Pistols of this type were made in the central and western Highlands, and may be regarded as a purely Highland type. They survived down to the middle of the XIXth century.

As the material used was, with rare exceptions,[8] steel, which was subsequently blued, the decoration applied to both the stocks and barrels was effected by the insetting of bands and panels of silver, the latter being in form circular, or of diamond- or heart-shape. The engraver's art was mostly applied to the silver surfaces. Here, again, the ornament consists of the leaf scroll and the rosette, but the thistle also appears. On a number of the pistols with the heart-shaped butt, made during the closing years of the XVIIth, or the very commencement of the XVIIIth century, appears the Dutch tulip (Plate V, Fig. 19), introduced with the accession to the British throne of William, Prince of Orange, an event which appealed to the feelings of the protestant Lowlander. Brass inlay is very rare. In the latest examples of this class the name of the maker, in place of mere initials, was sometimes engraved on the lock plate, and the date engraved there, on the fence, or along the top of the barrel.

In general these pistols were made in pairs, with right- and left-hand locks, and all had belt hooks and pickers. The picker and trigger terminals are ball-shaped, and sometimes the latter is in whole, or in part, of silver. The butts have a slight increase in the curve downwards from the stock. Plate IV, Fig. 16, shows a pistol with a form of butt which, in the writer's opinion, is unique at this period.

MECHANISM OF THE LATE SNAPHAUNCE LOCK

The locks of this class (Plate IV, Fig. 16) differ from those of the preceding class by the removal of the projecting nose of the sear (s), which now springs into a notch (N) in the tumbler (T). Otherwise the structure is the same, and suffers from the like defects (page 61, Fig. C).

The writer knows of only two guns with locks of this type: one is in Castle Grant and the other in Abbotsford.

CLASS II

THE FLINT-LOCK

Dated specimens show that this lock appeared first in 1665, and that it continued down to about 1820.

The final stage in the evolution of the lock of the Scottish pistol was the introduction of the flint-lock, which appeared in the third quarter of the XVIIth century. The left-hand locks were done away with by the close of the XVIIth century. The butts now show a more pronounced curve downwards, the proportions and finish become finer, and the engraving and inlay increase in amount and fineness. Silver and, in rare examples, brass or gold, are used for the inlay. Plate V, Fig. 19, shows a partially converted pistol of exceptional quality.

During the first half of the XVIIIth century the Highland pistol (scroll butt) was perfected, and showed a delicacy and elaboration of design and decoration which have caused Scottish pistols to be greatly sought after as objects of art. The form was gracefully proportioned, and the details finely finished, delicate fluting being applied to the breech end of the barrel and the scrolls of the butt, while the belt hooks are pierced and engraved. The whole surface is profusely engraved with scroll ornaments, and, in addition, in many cases the stock is inlaid with delicately intertwining lines of silver and, in rare instances, of gold; the ball terminals of trigger and picker being made of the same precious metal as the inlay (Plate VII, Figs. 24 and 25). The effect of this inlay work on the blue-black background is very striking. In rare instances the stock or barrel is made of brass. Many of the makers turned out pistols with a perforated disc or comb to the cock, a feature that evidently appeared shortly after 1700 (Plate VII, Fig. 24).

Type E. About the middle of the XVIIIth century there was introduced a type with a lobe-shaped butt (Plate VII, Fig. 28) similar to the conventional wood-stocked pistols of the period. These were made by the makers of the scroll-butt pattern, and were similarly finished, but had no picker fitted to the butt, and no perforated disc to the doghead. They were sometimes wholly of brass, particularly those made by T. Murdoch. The pistol maker did not confine himself to any uniform style of signature. For

K

instance John Murdoch signs indifferently *John Murdoch, Jo Murdoch*, IO MURDOCH, I MURDOCH, or MURDOCH, occasionally adding Doune, his town.

MECHANISM OF THE FLINT-LOCK. (CLASS II)

The conventional flint-lock was evolved by altering the form of the cock (c), combining the pan cover (PC) with the steel (ST), and inserting in the tumbler (T) the notches for the half and full cock (page 67, Fig. D). In the earliest specimens the dog-lock is found (Plate V, Fig. 18)—a small catch (HC) on the outside of the lock-plate fitting into a notch in the cock when drawn back to half cock, and being thrown out when the cock is drawn back to full cock.

The usual Scottish form of this fitting is a much smaller catch than that in the ordinary dog-lock (page 67, Fig. E).[9] Specimens are seldom met with.

In the pistols with the heart-shaped butt the trigger is, with a few exceptions, hung on a pin situated inside the stock, and screwed through the side of it to grip the strap of the belt hook.

The exceptions are a few fitted similarly to those of pistols with the scroll butt, where the pin, on which the trigger is hung, is screwed through the stock, above the lock plate. The top of the trigger projects upwards through a slot in the butt, is cut square and flush, and notched ornamentally.

With few exceptions the pistols manufactured in the Highlands show a reversion to the principle the snaphaunce (page 67, Fig. F), in that the nose of the sear (s) is elongated and projects through a square aperture in the lock plate, so as to grip the breast of the cock (c) at half cock. A spur on the rear of the sear snaps in over the tumbler (T), when put at full cock, thus withdrawing the nose from contact with the cock. This feature is rare in the pistols with the heart-shaped butt.

No bridle is found applied to the tumbler, but in some examples it is provided for the steel, by the elongation of the pan (Plate VIII, Fig. 30). The writer has found only one pistol with a rifled barrel. It is similar to Fig. 18 (Plate V), but the barrel is a plain tube moulded at the muzzle, and does not appear to be original.

All Scottish pistols are fitted with belt hooks, irrespective of the length of the pistol, which varies from 8 to 26 in.[10] The cost of a pair of

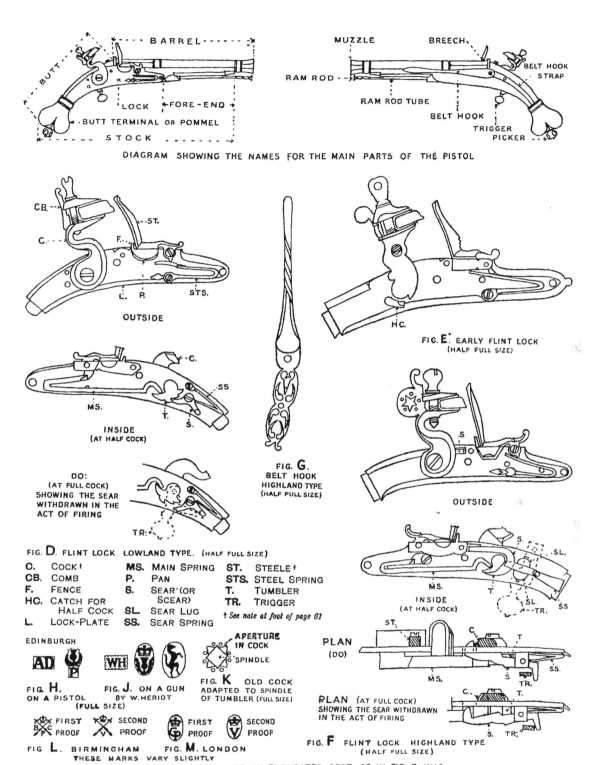

DIAGRAM SHOWING THE NAMES FOR THE MAIN PARTS OF THE PISTOL

OUTSIDE

INSIDE
(AT HALF COCK)

DO:
(AT FULL COCK)
SHOWING THE SEAR
WITHDRAWN IN THE
ACT OF FIRING

FIG. D. FLINT LOCK LOWLAND TYPE. (HALF FULL SIZE)

FIG. G.
BELT HOOK
HIGHLAND TYPE
(HALF FULL SIZE)

FIG. E. EARLY FLINT LOCK
(HALF FULL SIZE)

OUTSIDE

INSIDE
(AT HALF COCK)

PLAN
(DO)

PLAN (AT FULL COCK)
SHOWING THE SEAR WITHDRAWN
IN THE ACT OF FIRING

FIG. F FLINT LOCK HIGHLAND TYPE
(HALF FULL SIZE)

C.	COCK†	MS.	MAIN SPRING	ST. STEELE†
CB.	COMB	P.	PAN	STS. STEEL SPRING
F.	FENCE	S.	SEAR (OR SCEAR)	T. TUMBLER
HC.	CATCH FOR HALF COCK	SL.	SEAR LUG	TR. TRIGGER
L.	LOCK-PLATE	SS.	SEAR SPRING	† See note at foot of page 61

EDINBURGH

FIG. H.
ON A PISTOL
(FULL SIZE)

FIG. J. ON A GUN
BY W. HERIOT

FIG. K OLD COCK
ADAPTED TO SPINDLE
OF TUMBLER (FULL SIZE)

APERTURE
IN COCK
SPINDLE

FIRST PROOF · SECOND PROOF

FIRST PROOF · SECOND PROOF

FIG L. BIRMINGHAM   FIG. M. LONDON
THESE MARKS VARY SLIGHTLY

* AT A LATER DATE AN ELONGATED SEAR, AS IN FIG. F, WAS
FITTED, BUT, TO AVOID CONFUSION, THIS IS NOT SHOWN.
THIS LOCK IS SIGNED THOMAS CADDELL 1678

DIAGRAMS OF THE FLINT LOCK

Highland pistols in Doune, Perthshire, about 1798, varied, according to quality, from 4 to 24 guineas.[11]

The illustrations in this section show only the finest specimens of their class. The smaller makers turned out quite interesting pieces of ruder finish, examples of which are not so often found.

Plate VIII shows two particularly fine examples of the Highland pistol at its best. Although one, the earlier, was made in Doune (Fig. 29), and the other in Stirling (Fig. 30), they appear to be by the same maker.

The Scottish pistol-making industry died out with the XVIIIth century, receiving its death-blow from the importation of cheap English-made pistols. These pistols are a clumsy imitation. Some are stocked in silver, or white composition metal, but the cheaper qualities are made of malleable cast iron. They were in use as an article of ceremonial Highland dress down to about 1850, and bear the name of the gunmaker, or accoutrement maker, who sold them (Plate VII, Figs. 26 and 27).

These costume pistols, although they vary considerably in quality, must not be confounded with the original models, from which they are easily distinguished by keeping in mind several points of deviation.

They have the usual form of cock used in ordinary firearms of the first quarter of the XIXth century; the scrolls of the butt are too thin; the muzzle wants the quick turn up at the extremity; the terminal of the trigger is a clumsy steel knob, while that of the picker takes a poppy head or thistle form. These terminals are sometimes mounted with coloured natural crystals. In some examples an attempt has been made to reproduce the cock with the perforated disc, but the result is clumsy and disproportionate. The decoration of the stock and barrel consists of scroll forms, trophies of arms, thistles, or the figure of St. Andrew, executed by acid embossing or engraving, fire gilt in places. The lock is engraved also.

The difference between the engraving on the costume pistol, and its immediate precursor, lies in the more graceful flowing lines and deeper cutting of the earlier work. The points of the leaf scrolls are cut deeper than the rest of the scroll, and hatched to accentuate still further the forms, this being necessary to obtain a crisp effect on the dark surface. The engraving on the lock is usually slightly shallower. On the costume pistol the engraving is evenly cut throughout, while the ornament is, as a rule, stiffer, giving a hard appearance.

Another point to note is that these late reproductions bear the Birmingham proof marks on the barrels, for which reference is directed to page 67, Fig. L. It cannot be said, with any certainty, whether these pistols were made and finished in Birmingham, or merely made there and engraved and finished in Scotland.

The very latest examples have the contemporary percussion lock, and appear to have been made down to about 1850 when their manufacture ceased completely.

In closing this review of a very interesting development in the history of European firearms, the writer would cite, as the outstanding feature of Scottish firearms, the general use of metal, particularly of steel, in the formation of pistol stocks. Metal was very rarely employed abroad, and was there limited almost exclusively to the short, heavy, wheel-lock pistols, with steel stocks, made in Germany in the XVIth century.

Whether this preference for the use of metal, on the part of the Scottish pistol makers, arose from the demands of public taste, or the difficulty of obtaining suitable wood, is a matter of indifference. The fact remains that they chose the most difficult material to work, and consequently all the more credit is due to them for the excellent results which they achieved.

It can justly be claimed for the Scottish gun and pistol makers of the period from the XVIth to the XVIIIth century, that they evolved weapons unique in form and decoration, and quite unlike anything produced elsewhere at similar periods. Although it may be objected that their handiwork is inferior in elaboration and artistic excellence to the products of the great Continental gunsmiths, yet no one can justly deny them the right to take their stand, as craftsmen and artists, alongside those of any other country.

GUNS AND PISTOLS OF THE GENERAL CONVENTIONAL PATTERN MADE IN SCOTLAND

THE guns and pistols of the general conventional pattern produced in Scotland were similar to those made in England at the same period (XVIIIth and XIXth centuries), the only difference, where they show any, is in small matters of detail, such as the curve of the cock, or the design and execution of the engraving.

In the earlier examples the whole piece was of native workmanship, but probably, early in the last quarter of the XVIIIth century, the practice came into use of importing the barrels from England. Nearly all the firearms of this description, which the writer has examined, belonging to the last quarter of the XVIIIth century, and all of those made during the first half of the XIXth century, have barrels bearing the proof marks of Birmingham or London (see page 67, Figs. L and M). The locks and stocks were made and fitted in Scotland, but gun makers in a small way merely assembled apparently the parts purchased from the manufacturers in Birmingham, and fitted the stocks; while merchants, such as ironmongers, sold firearms imported complete, either with no signature, or with the names of these ironmongers or agents engraved in Birmingham upon the pieces.

It is illegal to sell in England any unproved firearm, *i.e.*, any gun or pistol that has not passed the tests of the Proof Houses of London or Birmingham, but as these Proof Houses have no jurisdiction in Scotland, which has no Proof House of its own, it has always been, and still is, possible to sell unproved firearms in Scotland.

It is evident, however, that at least in Edinburgh there was some form of proof carried out by the gun makers, who were a section of the Incorporation of Hammermen. The business books of the "Darien Company" contain several entries about 1700 regarding the proving of firearms purchased locally

71

for the Company's use.[12]   What the proof mark was, and when it came into use, are matters which are not clear, for on two pieces in the writer's collection, which are also the only examples so marked which he has met with, the marks differ.   One is a flint-lock pistol with a cannon barrel and stock of walnut with steel mounts.   The period of it is the middle of the XVIIIth century.   The barrel bears, at the breech, the maker's initials [A.D.] and a proof mark (see page 67, Fig. H).   The other is a single-barrel, flint-lock fowling piece, with walnut stock and brass mounts, signed W. HERIOT, EDINBURGH.   The barrel is slightly bell-mouthed and bears, at the breech, the maker's initials, the Scottish National emblem (the thistle), and the hind, the emblem of St. Giles, the patron saint of Edinburgh.   The first Edinburgh Directory published in 1773 shows that Heriot was in business then (see page 67, Fig. J).

The flint-lock fowling pieces, with single or double barrels, made during the last quarter of the XVIIIth century and first quarter of the XIXth, were in quality and finish equal to those made in England during the same period.

A great change came with the invention of the percussion lock in 1805 by the Rev. Alexander John Forsyth, M.A., LL.D., parish minister of Belhelvie, Aberdeenshire.[13] Although his patent was taken out on 4 July 1807, the invention did not come into general use till about the beginning of the second quarter of the XIXth century, when a great number of flint-lock firearms was converted to the new system.

CRAFTSMANSHIP

THERE are several points to be noted with regard to the craftsmanship and mode of construction of the Scottish pistol of the national type where metal is solely employed. The barrel and lock were probably made first, and the stock fitted afterwards. The brass barrel was cast, the bore drilled out to the required diameter, and the exterior filed down to form parts such as the raised bands. How the earlier steel barrels were formed is not evident, but the later ones, of the XVIIIth century, were made by what is known as "plain twist" (the common mode in use elsewhere at that time). In this process a long steel ribbon was welded up, preferably out of old horseshoe nails, and then hammered round an iron rod, or mandril, in a close spiral twist. The barrel was then heated to a welding heat, and the joints welded. After that it was again heated sufficiently to allow of the mandrel being driven out. The bore was then drilled out to the required diameter, and the outer surface filed down, the breech end tapped with a thread, and the breech plug screwed in. The writer has a pair of pistols by John Campbell of Doune, where the bore shows clearly the spiral line of the edges of the ribbon. The touch hole is in rare examples found bushed with brass, but this appears to have been done only after the hole had become too large, through corrosion by the powder; and was not a feature of the weapon when it was originally made.

The old locks were made differently from the modern ones, for in those days material was dear and labour cheap; conditions which are now reversed. Moreover, the modern maker has machinery and a large variety of fine tools, easily procurable from the merchants, and the best steel in a variety of sizes; but the early worker had to make his own tools, and had few of them. It is found therefore that those early locks are of the simplest construction. The component parts were very neatly forged by the hammer, so as to get as near as possible to the final dimensions, and thereby reduced to a minimum the

L

loss of material, and the tear and wear of the tools which were employed in the finishing of the surfaces with the file. A manufacturing gun maker, after examining an exceptionally fine pistol of the Highland type by one of the best makers, has remarked that the filing up of the external part of the lock was most beautifully done, and would tax the skill of the best men in the trade to-day. Those early craftsmen were deficient in the designing, finishing and fitting of the working parts of the interior of the lock, which wanted a bridle, and thus caused an uneven working of the tumbler and much friction. The tempering of the springs left much to be desired. The silver ball terminals of the triggers and pickers were made hollow and in halves, an upper and lower, which were soldered together and slipped on to the iron tang of the trigger or picker, the extremity of which was then riveted neatly over (*see* Plate VI, Fig. 23).

The metal stocks were made in one piece. The material was first beaten out to the proper thickness, cut to the required dimensions, and then hammered into the ultimate form. The globose, or heart-shaped, butt terminal was forged in two sections and brazed together, then riveted to the butt end of the stock, and brazed on. In the case of a steel globose butt terminal, of octagonal section, on a pistol in the writer's collection, the joining is across the centre of the terminal, and there is a dovetail joint in each face. In the case of the heart-shaped butt the joining is longitudinal along the upper and lower edges. In the scroll butt type the stock is still in one piece, the only joining being where the outer face is folded over to complete the butt and brazed to the flange on the under side. The scroll terminal is forged in one piece and brazed to the end of the butt. The writer has seen several pistols in which the butts have been made with a "cast-off," that is, a slight curve to the right to counteract the tendency to fire towards the left, caused by the release of the tumbler on pressing the trigger.

THE APPLICATION OF SURFACE DECORATION

The brass pistol is composed of a material which lends itself to the engraver's art, and hence the profusion of such decoration. The steel pistol is made of a material difficult for the graver's tool, and the blueing of the surface to prevent rusting reduced the effectiveness of the incised work and induced the application of an inlay consisting of a metal of light colour. The inlay was an insetting of thin silver plates, fixed as follows. The area to be occupied was sunk to the thickness of the plate, the edges undercut and raised. The plate was then packed into its place, and the raised edges beaten down over it. The narrow intertwining lines were cut into the steel and slightly dovetailed. The metal for the inlay was cut into thin strips and beaten into the channel.

HINTS TO COLLECTORS

 COLLECTOR has always to be wary lest he be deceived by a reproduction of an antique example or a genuinely old specimen which has been tampered with. Such examples must not be confused with cases showing the repairs, renewals, or conversions naturally found on weapons that have been in continual service over a long period, during which various systems of lock have been introduced. Conversions are most commonly found during the transition from the late snaphaunce to the flint-lock.

The archaeologist and connoisseur is born, not made. The most competent judge of the antique is he who, born with the gift of discrimination, has cultivated it, not only by the study of books and photographs, but, most necessary of all, by the careful study of the actual objects. A great deal can be learned by taking to pieces even a few firearms, and by cleaning and putting them together again; also, by supervising the gun maker who carries out any necessary repairs, by noting how he executes the work and observing the tool marks which he leaves, so that they may be compared with those found on the old work. The parts most commonly lost are the ramrod and picker—which may work loose and fall out unnoticed. The cock is the part most frequently found broken, on account of the thin curved neck which easily snaps if the pistol falls with this part undermost on, say, a stone floor. These parts are, therefore, occasionally found to be of later date and out of keeping with the rest of the weapon.

The successful detection of a cock that is not original calls for the careful consideration of the shape, style of engraving, and mode of attachment. The cock may be of much later date than the pistol, and consequently be of a different form from the original. It might have the form of that on Plate VII, Fig. 26, whereas it ought to be similar to that on Plate VII, Fig. 25. When the form of the cock is similar to the original the engraving may, in style or execution, give the true period of the part, or the cock may be too long or too short to articulate properly with the steel. Another test in a doubtful case is to remove the pin which holds the cock to the tumbler, to see whether the square aperture fits correctly on to the spindle. In a case of substitution the cock sometimes requires that the aperture be cut to fit. If, however, the aperture be too large it becomes necessary to spread out the sides by striking the required spot with a pointed punch, thus expanding the metal sufficiently to receive the new notches; for which see page 67, Fig. K.

Care should be taken to retain the cock in position. If it be removed the lock will fly asunder on account of there being no bridle to hold the mechanism together. The pins or screws should also be examined, because the early ones were hand cut, and consequently the thread is wider in spacing, slightly uneven, and shallow in the cutting.

The conversion of a lock from one system to another certainly reduces the value of the weapon, but it does not necessarily rule out the specimen as a collector's piece. Such an alteration can be detected by a careful examination of the lock plate for old holes that have been plugged, which show the position of the original parts (Plate V, Fig. 19).

It sometimes happens that the whole lock is not original, but has been correctly made for, and fitted to, an old stock. In such a case the toolmarks, the pins, and the execution of the decoration are the only guides. If, however, as most often happens, it is an old lock taken from another piece, an examination of the lock and its attachment to the stock may show where adjusting alterations have been made, or that the touch hole in the barrel is not in proper relation to the pan.

It is rare to find a pistol with a barrel of a later date, but such a case might quite naturally occur through the bursting of the original barrel. It is worth noting that the writer has on one or two occasions come across Highland pistols of the late XVIIIth century that had been sent at a later time to Birmingham to have the barrels proved. The proof marks had been struck after the engraving had been done. Therefore the barrels had not been proved at the time when they were manufactured.

RESTORATION OF FIREARMS

ESTORATION is a process that must be applied to objects of antiquity with very careful forethought. Firstly, it has to be considered whether it is advisable to attempt restoration at all; secondly, how much restoration should be undertaken; thirdly, how it can be carried out most conservatively and efficiently. There is one general principle that should never be departed from, and that is, that all original parts should be retained and carefully cleaned, but no touching up of the engraving or interference with the original work should be permitted. Any new work added should be done in such a way that, while the whole piece would appear homogeneous, a close inspection would clearly show what is old and what is new. The following is an instance of a restoration carried out on correct lines. A pistol came into the possession of the writer which was seen to have been clumsily converted about 1800 from a snaphaunce to a flint-lock, the trigger having been cut down to suit, and a trigger guard and a new ramrod of the crudest description fitted. The restoration removed these unsightly modern additions, and replaced them with parts correctly reproduced from contemporary specimens. The lock plate, the only original part of the lock remaining, has not been touched, except for the necessary plugging of the modern pin holes and the bushing and retapping of the original pin holes, which had been plugged when the pistol was converted. The new parts were carefully copied from another similar pistol, and browned with acid, but no engraving or pitting of the surface to imitate the effect of age was attempted. Thus the effect of the original weapon is obtained, and yet the new work is quite easily distinguishable.

The actual work of the restoration was carried out by a skilled, practical gun maker, working to carefully prepared full-size drawings of every part, executed by the writer, who also supervised the work. The cost, however, was very high—about £20—owing to the time occupied, a gun maker being unaccustomed to work from drawings. In such a case as this it would have been more satisfactory to have had the pieces made in wood by a model maker, which would have allowed of the whole work being checked before its final execution in metal. It would also have saved time and expense.

Another case in which restoration should be carried out is where a part, or parts, of the original lock are missing, and data are available from other examples by the same or another contemporary maker, which would allow of an absolutely correct restoration being carried out. For example: The unsightly ramrod should be removed from the pistol shown in Plate IV, Fig. 13, and a correct reproduction fitted. Similarly, Plate IV, Fig. 16, shows a modern steel loop screwed into the barrel to hold the ramrod. This should be removed and a metal tube of correct design fitted.

Restoration work must always be placed in the hands of a highly skilled, intelligent craftsman, working under the supervision of someone thoroughly conversant with all the details of the ancient work and the methods that produced it. Not only so, but where new parts have to be designed, on the lines of what is extant, it calls for an aptitude in visualizing what was in the mind of the original designer. If the possessor of a defective firearm cannot do this, or grudges the necessary outlay, he would be well advised to leave it alone. The writer has seen some abominable work of this kind done by those who should have known better.

NOTES

(1). The match-lock was doubtless made in Scotland, although the writer has, so far, not found any examples.

To show the extent of the overlap of types the following instances may be cited :

Among the locks of Class I (the snaphaunce) an example is shown of the early type dated 1686 (Plate I, Fig. 4), while the late type appears in a specimen dated as early as 1647 (Plate IV, Fig. 16).

In the transition from Class I to Class II (the flint-lock) the same feature appears, for the writer has in his collection a late snaphaunce lock dated 1702, while the early flint-lock is illustrated by a specimen dated 1678 (page 67, Fig. E).

(2). The musket has a bore of twelve leaden bullets to the pound. The arquebus is of smaller bore, about sixteen or more bullets to the pound. Hence " 12 bore " and " 16 bore."

(3).

The Countess of Seafield, Castle Grant, Morayshire (of which three are rifles)	13
The Duke of Montrose, Buchanan Castle, Stirlingshire	1
J. Scott Maxwell, Esq., Abbotsford, Roxburghshire	1
R. L. Scott, Esq., Greenock	1
Alfred W. Cox, Esq., Glendoick, Perthshire	1
The United Service Institution, London	1
The Tower Armoury, London	3
	21

(4). The writer possesses the barrel of a similar musket. It has three inset bands of brass inscribed MARIA and JESUS, and, along the top, inlaid in brass, W. G. OF GYCHT 1555 5 OCTR. (William Gordon of Gight, in Aberdeenshire).

(5). In the Museum, Dresden, are three pairs of pistols with wooden stocks and fish-tail butts. The earliest pair has no mounts and is engraved only on the working parts of the locks, but otherwise is finely finished. The locks are signed I H and dated 1598, which makes them the earliest known firearm of Scottish make, and also places them amongst the earliest examples of a firearm on this principle. One of the pairs has steel barrels blued and gilt, and another has a loop of cord with a tassel attached to go over the wrist, in the same manner as a present-day cavalry soldier secures his sabre.

(6). The writer possesses the only example he has met with of a pistol of Class I with a steel stock and globose butt. The stock is quite plain, but the lock plate, being of brass, is decorated. It is dated 1634.

(7). When Richard Cameron the covenanter was killed at the battle of Airs Moss in 1680, he is described as having had a couple of steel pistols attached to his wrists.

M

(8). There is one wholly of brass and engraved throughout, in the Kelvingrove Museum, Glasgow. The writer has seen several with brass barrels.

(9). On a steel pistol with scroll butt. Signed Thomas Caddell 1678. In the Museum, Neuchâtel, Switzerland.

(10). This is the longest example the writer knows of. It has a flint-lock and a heart-shaped butt. The date is about 1700, although the barrel looks older. It is in the Antiquarian Museum Perth.

(11). See " The Statistical Account of Scotland," 1798, vol. 20, page 86.

(12). The Journal of the Court of Directors of the Company of Scotland (" The Darien Company "), preserved in the Royal Bank of Scotland, Edinburgh, contains several entries similar to the following :

" Edinburgh, 27th day of August 1697.
" Ordered—That Baillie Hugh Cunningham oversee the proving of the Fuzees made by John Simpson Gunsmith for the Company's use."

(13). " The Rev. Alexander John Forsyth, M.A., LL.D.," by Major-General Sir Alexander J. Forsyth Reid, K.C.B., M.A., LL.D. The University Press, Aberdeen, 1910.

NOTE ON THE INCORPORATIONS OF HAMMERMEN IN SCOTLAND

THE two inventions, early in the XVIth century, on the Continent, of the wheel-lock and snaphaunce respectively, marked an enormous advance in the perfecting of hand fire-arms. These two new ideas were great improvements on the earlier match-lock which was, however, a less costly mechanism and was hence continued in use well into the XVIIth century.

Probably shortly after the application of the two new ideas to firearms abroad the wheel-lock and snaphaunce were introduced into Scotland, and examples would naturally be much appreciated and sought after in that warlike country by those who could afford to purchase them. The Scottish artificers would, of course, be called upon to effect repairs to these new types of weapons, and the more skilled native craftsmen would therefore be employed. The more enterprising and skilful among these men would naturally take up this repair work and, if successful in this, would eventually begin to copy at least the less intricate of the two mechanisms, viz., the snaphaunce, and produce complete weapons. The engraver would also apply his art to the embellishment of the native-made specimens, using the style of decoration that was in vogue in Scotland at that particular time and which they were accustomed to use every day.

No evidence has yet been obtained that the wheel-lock was made in Scotland.

It may be safely stated that the manufacture of snaphaunce firearms was being gradually introduced into Scotland at a time not later than the middle of the XVIth century. Previous to about the year 1587 the makers of firearms in Scotland do not appear to have been recognized as a separate craft, but to have been included among the members of one or other of the crafts dealing with similar productions, such as locks and clocks. It was evidently the increasing importance of the industry which eventually demanded its recognition and its elevation to the status of a separate craft, for by the beginning of the third quarter of the XVIth century gun- and dag-making had reached a stage of almost full development.

A barrel of a heavy wall-piece, dated 1555, in the writer's possession (see Note 4), exhibits all the characteristics of the developed Scottish work which are shown by two pieces of the XVIth century, one a musket dated 1599 (see page 59), and the other a dag, signed I.K. and dated 1598 (see List of Makers).

Supporting these facts and deductions are the following pieces of information gleaned from old records touching upon the affairs of the makers of firearms in four of the leading Scottish towns.

In the Burgh Records of St. Andrews, entered prior to the year 1600, are the names of two dagmakers. The earlier entry is dated 1585.

The " Lockit Book " of the Incorporation of Hammermen of Dundee was commenced in the year 1587, and contains a list of the master craftsmen, including eight "gunmakers," who already in that year were following their trade. Down to the year 1600 eight new gunmakers had been admitted, and thirteen apprentices had been indentured, the first three in 1588.

The Records of the Incorporation of Hammermen of Edinburgh commence in 1494, and the names of "dagmakers" first appear there in the year 1588. The Edinburgh Guild Register of Apprentices shows that down to the year 1600 at least five "dagmakers" were there practising their craft, the earliest reference being in 1588, and that six apprentices, the first also in 1588, had been indentured.

The Burgess Roll of Aberdeen contains mention of a "gunmaker" in 1591 who had in his charge for the previous year the ". . . keeping of the thre knok [clocks]. . . ."

It may be noted that the terms "dagmakers," "gunmaker," and "gunsmith," apparently refer to men carrying out the same work, and may be looked upon as synonymous, for in the Dundee records are two entries in which the same man is referred to as a "gunmaker" in the one, and a "dagmaker" in the other.

It would be futile at this stage to attempt to identify the gun and pistol makers who signed merely with initials, but after the names of these craftsmen, working in all the principal towns in Scotland, have been obtained, other evidence may also have come to light making it possible to write on these men and their activities with more confidence.

DESCRIPTION OF PLATES

PLATE I

1. SMALL ARQUEBUS, with early snaphaunce lock (imperfect), finely engraved with leaf scrolls. The lock plate and pan are of brass, the former stamped with the maker's initials, R.A., and the latter engraved on the fence with the date 1614. The works are of steel. The barrel has several raised moulded bands and is engraved, mostly at the muzzle. The maker's initials and date are repeated at the breech. The stock is of rosewood, inlaid in silver with thistle heads and leaves, and fitted with a trigger guard.

    Length, 4 ft. 2½ in.

    This piece is said to have been made for King Charles I.

    Preserved in the Armoury of the Tower, London.

2. ARQUEBUS, with early snaphaunce lock, signed AP and dated 1635. See enlargement and full description of this piece on Plate II, Fig. 7.

3. ARQUEBUS, with early snaphaunce lock, finely engraved with leaf scrolls. The lock plate is stamped with the maker's initials, I.S., surmounted by a crown of three points. The barrel, octagonal, inlaid with silver bands, bears the arms of James, fifth Earl and first Marquis of Montrose (executed in 1650), and his initials, I.E.M. Engraved across the breech is the incomplete date 16.... The stock is of walnut, carved and fluted, and fitted with an engraved brass butt plate.

    Length, 5 ft. 1¾ in.

    The property of the Duke of Montrose.

    Note.—Half of the fore end of the stock is broken away.

4. BREECH-LOADING RIFLE, with early snaphaunce lock, finely engraved on the working parts with leaf scroll ornament, signed G.S., and dated on the fence 1686. The barrel is octagonal and rifled with eight grooves ; it screws asunder in front of the lock plate to allow of the

charge being inserted. The stock is of beech, fluted and delicately carved with running leaf scrolls and grotesque animals. The trigger has a steel ball terminal but no guard.

Length, 4 ft. 7½ in.

The property of the Countess of Seafield.

PLATE II

5. ARQUEBUS, with early snaphaunce lock, engraved with leaf ornament and grotesque animals. It bears the maker's signature, $ JNVERNES, and is dated on the fence 1684. There is a bridle to the steel, but no buffer to the cock. The trigger has lost its silver ball terminal and has no trigger guard. The barrel is circular, finely fluted at the breech, and inlaid with engraved silver panels. There is a similar band of silver round the muzzle. The stock is of beech, finely fluted and mounted with silver; the butt plate is missing.

Length, 5 ft. 3¾ in. Bore, $\frac{11}{16}$ in.

The property of the Countess of Seafield.

6. MUSKET, with early snaphaunce lock, finely engraved and signed GULIELMUS SMITH, BELLACHASTEL. There is no buffer to the cock. The barrel is circular, except towards the breech, where it is octagonal; the surface is finely channelled and has a raised comb running out to the muzzle. The stock is of beech, finely fluted and slightly curved, and the mounts are of brass; the butt plate is missing. The trigger has been changed, and a trigger guard added in the following century. Another gun by this maker in the same collection bears the date 1674.

Length, 5 ft. 9¾ in. Bore, ¾ in.

The property of the Countess of Seafield.

7. ARQUEBUS, with early snaphaunce lock, finely engraved with leaf scrolls. The lock plate is of brass stamped with the maker's initials, A.P.; the works are of steel (partly restored), and bear the date 1635 on the fence. The barrel is in parts finely fluted and inlaid with engraved bands and plaques of silver and brass. It bears the following

inscription: DOMINUS JOHANNES GRANT MILES VICECOMES DE INNERNES ME FECIT IN GERMANIA ANNO 1434 (Sir John Grant, Knight, Sheriff of Inverness, made me in Germany in the year 1434) (the latter part of this inscription is fictitious); also the coat-of-arms, with "S.I.G. of Freuchy K." (Sir John Grant of Freuchy, Knight), repeated on the butt plate. The stock is of ~~walnut~~, fluted and ornamented with applied figures in silver—the lion and unicorn, man on horseback, dogs, fish, and small placques.

Length, 5 ft. 4 in. Bore, $\frac{5}{8}$ in.

The property of the Countess of Seafield.

Note.—The upper jaw and pin of the cock and the steel have been restored. The restored parts of the cock are inaccurate, and should have been similar to Plate IV, Fig. 12.

PLATE III

8. DAG, or pistol, wholly of brass with early snaphaunce lock; the lock plate, bearing the maker's stamp ♭, is of brass, and the works are of steel. The barrel and stock are finely engraved with leaf scrolls. The barrel has raised moulded bands and the stock terminates in a flat butt finished in a fish-tail form.

   This specimen, along with others in the same collection, may have been taken to the Continent by Scottish soldiers of fortune, many of whom served under Gustavus Adolphus in the Thirty Years' War.

   A similar pistol, dated 1613, by this maker is in the Zeughaus, Berlin.

   Preserved in the Royal Armoury, Stockholm.

9. DAG, or pistol, left-handed, with early snaphaunce lock (incomplete). The lock is of steel, exceptionally well executed and finely engraved on the working parts. It is stamped with the maker's initials, MM. The steel and buffer are missing. The barrel is of steel, ornamented with raised moulded crossbands enclosing bands of engraved silver. The muzzle is octagonal, and slightly bell-mouthed. The stock is of

walnut, mounted with silver, finely engraved with floral and leaf scrolls, and terminates in a flat butt with a mount of fish-tail form. The butt is fitted with a picker with a button-shaped terminal of silver. The trigger is ball-shaped at the extremity. The ramrod is missing, but was originally of steel. This with the missing parts of the lock were similar to those in Plate IV, Fig. 15. Date about 1650.

Length, 15⅞ in.

Preserved in the Royal Scottish Museum, Edinburgh.

10. DAG, or pistol, wholly of steel, with late snaphaunce lock, showing slight traces of engraving. The date is on the fence, 166- (the last figure has disappeared). The barrel is octagonal. The stock is plain, and terminates in a flat butt, finished with a scroll terminal fitted with a picker, which is a clumsy modern restoration. This piece has suffered severely from overcleaning.

Length, 16½ in. (excluding picker).

Preserved in the Armoury of the Tower, London.

11. DAG, or pistol, left-hand, with early snaphaunce lock, finely engraved. The lock plate and pan are of brass, the former stamped with the maker's initials, C.A.; the latter bearing on the fence the date 1619. The comb of the cock is broken away. (See Plate IV, Fig. 12.) The works are of steel. The barrel is of steel, moulded at the muzzle, engraved at the breech, and dated 1619. The stock is of walnut, with finely engraved mounts and inlaid straps of brass in the form of thistles and rosettes. It has a steel ramrod. The butt is flat, terminating in a mount of fish-tail form. It was not fitted with a picker.

Length, 16⅜ in.

Preserved in the Armoury of the Tower, London.

PLATE IV

12. DAG, or pistol, with early snaphaunce lock, finely engraved with leaf ornament. The lock plate is of brass, stamped with the maker's initials, R.M., and the works are of steel. The barrel is of brass, with moulded muzzle and crossbands, the upper surface being engraved

with interlaced bands enclosing panels of leaf ornament, finishing at the muzzle with the Scottish thistle, displayed. It bears the date 1625 across the breech. The stock is of walnut without mounts, and terminates in a lemon-shaped butt, which is not fitted with a picker. The decoration is restricted to incised lines and dots. The ramrod is missing, but was originally of wood, probably tipped with bone

Length, 15 in. Bore, $\frac{7}{16}$ in.

The property of C. E. Whitelaw, Esq., F.S.A.Scot.

13. DAG, or pistol, wholly of brass, with early snaphaunce lock. It is engraved throughout with leaf scrolls and interlaced work. The lock plate is of brass stamped with the maker's initials, A.C., and the pan and works are of steel. The barrel is ornamented with raised moulded bands, and dated across the breech 1634. The butt is of flattened lemon shape, fitted with a perforated steel picker. The ramrod is very much later, and was originally similar to that of Plate IV, Fig. 14.

This pistol is one of a pair with right- and left-hand locks.

Length, 16¾ in.

The property of the University of Aberdeen.

14. DAG, or pistol, left-handed, of brass and steel, with early snaphaunce lock. The lock plate is of brass, engraved with leaf scrolls, and stamped with the maker's initials, I.C. The works are of steel. The buffer is missing. The barrel is of steel with raised moulded bands, and has an octagonal muzzle. The stock is of brass, engraved with leaf scrolls and interlaced strapwork, and terminated by a globose butt, pierced and fitted with a perforated picker. The steel parts are much corroded. Date about 1650.

Length, 13 in.

Unearthed near the site of Partick Castle, Glasgow.

Preserved in Kelvingrove Museum, Glasgow.

15. DAG, or pistol, left-handed, with early snaphaunce lock. The lock and barrel are of steel, without decoration. The comb is broken away from the cock, but was probably similar to that of Plate IV, Fig. 13. The barrel is polygonal at breech and muzzle, the latter being slightly bell-mouthed. The stock is of walnut with brass mount, finished by

a brass butt terminal of octagonal lemon shape, which has not been fitted with a picker. The ramrod is of steel. This pistol was discovered in 1849 while demolishing an old house at No. 71 Saltmarket, Glasgow. Date about 1650.

Length, 15⅝ in.

The property of N. R. Colville, Esq., F.S.A.Scot.

16. DAG, or pistol, left-handed, wholly of steel, with late snaphaunce lock. The lock is unsigned, and the decoration of leaf scrolls is limited to the works. The fence bears the date 1647—very early for this type of lock. The barrel has raised moulded crossbands enclosing engraved bands of silver, and an octagonal muzzle. The stock is plain, terminating in a lobe-shaped butt, a form unique at this period. The butt was fitted with a picker (now missing). The steel loop holding the ramrod is modern. These fittings in their original form would be similar to those on Plate IV, Fig. 14.

Length, 16¼ in.

The property of N. R. Colville, Esq., F.S.A.Scot.

PLATE V

17. DAG, or pistol, left-handed, wholly of steel, with late snaphaunce lock. The lock plate bears the initials of the maker, — S. (which may have stood for William Smith), and the works are engraved with leaf scrolls, and are dated on the fence 1671. The barrel is absolutely plain except for an inset silver plate. The stock is quite plain and finished by a heart-shaped terminal.

Length, 20¼ in.

The property of the Countess of Seafield.

18. PISTOL, wholly of steel, with early flint-lock. The lock is of the type known as a " dog-lock," *i.e.*, it is fitted with a small outside catch to retain the cock at half cock. The works are engraved with leaf scrolls, but there is no signature or date. The pin of the cock is later. The barrel has moulded crossbands enclosing inset bands of silver, and

an octagonal muzzle. The stock is plain and finished by a heart-shaped butt terminal, which has not been fitted with the usual picker. This piece has suffered severely from overcleaning. A similar, but slightly earlier pistol, in Mr. Colville's collection, is dated 1665.

Length, 10¼ in.

The property of C. E. Whitelaw, Esq., F.S.A.Scot.

19.   DAG, or pistol, wholly of steel, with a very late snaphaunce lock converted to flint-lock. It is a piece of exceptional quality.

The lock is engraved with leaf scroll ornament, and bears the initials of the maker, D.H. The cock has a comb of finely pierced scrollwork, but unfortunately has been broken and spliced below the neck. The fence is large and circular, with a sunk panel filled in with delicate filigree work in brass. The steel has been originally similar in form to that of Plate V, Fig. 17, but at a later date the pan cover was removed and a new steel and spring of the flint-lock pattern fitted by an inferior craftsman. The barrel has the usual raised cross mouldings enclosing engraved silver bands, the spaces between being inlaid with intertwined stems of brass connecting rosettes, thistles, and tulips inlaid in silver. The compartment next the breech is filled in with a diaper of inlaid and engraved diamond-shaped plaques of silver. The stock is finished with a heart-shaped butt terminal, and both are decorated similarly to the barrel. The belt hook has a large circular disc at the upper end, with open-work spirals on either side, and is decorated with a sunk panel of delicate filigree work in brass similar to the fence. The strap terminates in fine open scroll-work. The ramrod and tube are late unsightly restorations, and the picker is missing. The stock is inscribed:

"Ex DONO IA D DE HAMILTON [from a gift by James, Duke of Hamilton]. PAT LUNDIN. JAMES LUNDIN. James Grahame his noball arm given to him by . . . Daneile esquire."

This duke succeeded to the title in 1698.

Length, 20⅜ in.   Bore, ⅝ in.

Preserved in the Royal Scottish Museum, Edinburgh.

PLATE VI

FIG.

20. PISTOL, wholly of steel, with flint-lock. The lock is engraved with leaf scrolls and signed ALEX^R SHIRES, OLD MELDRUM. The sear projects through the lock plate after the fashion of the Highland locks, which is not usual in this type of pistol. The barrel is profusely inlaid with fine intertwined lines and crossbands, diamond-shaped and circular discs, and a broad band round the muzzle, all of engraved silver. It bears near the breech the date 1700. The stock is plain, except for engraved silver crossbands on the under side, and is finished by a heart-shaped butt terminal, engraved and inlaid with silver. It is fitted with a perforated picker.

Length, 16¼ in.   Bore, $\frac{9}{16}$ in.

This is one of a pair in exceptionally fine preservation in the Royal Scottish Museum, Edinburgh.

21. PISTOL, wholly of steel, with flint-lock. The lock is plain, signed DAVID MCKENZIE, and punched with the pot of lilies—the insignia of the town of Dundee. The barrel is ornamented with raised moulded crossbands, enclosing inset bands of rudely engraved silver, the intervening spaces being filled in with the crowned thistle, heart- and diamond-shaped panels, etc., similarly executed. The stock is inlaid with rudely engraved bands of silver, and is finished by a heart-shaped butt terminal inlaid with scroll lines of silver. The picker is not original and the ramrod is missing: these fittings would be similar to those in Plate VI, Fig. 20. First quarter of XVIIIth century.

Length, 9½ in.

Preserved in the Albert Institute, Dundee.

22. PISTOL, wholly of steel, with flint-lock, of rather rude workmanship. The lock is engraved with scroll ornament, and signed THOS. CADDELL (Doune). The cock is not original, although correct in form. The barrel and stock are ornamented with inlaid bands and circular and heart-shaped plaques of engraved silver. The butt is flat and

finished by a scroll terminal, fitted with a picker which, with the trigger, is mounted with a pierced ball terminal of silver. The ramrod and tube are a late restoration, and were originally similar to those of Plate VII, Fig. 24. Date about 1700.

Length, 15¾ in.

Preserved in the Natural History and Antiquarian Museum, Montrose.

23. PISTOL, wholly of steel, with flint-lock. The lock is engraved with scroll ornament and has the perforated disc to the cock. Signed ALEXANDER CAMERON. The barrel is fluted at the breech and has an octagonal muzzle slightly bell-mouthed. The surface is engraved in places with scroll ornament. The stock is also engraved with scroll ornament, and has a flat butt with a scroll terminal. The belt hook is pierced and engraved. The trigger and picker terminals are of silver. The ramrod is missing, but would be similar to that of Plate VII, Fig. 24. First quarter of XVIIIth century.

Length, 15⅝ in.

Property of N. R. Colville, Esq., F.S.A.Scot.

PLATE VII

24. PISTOL, wholly of steel, with flint-lock. The lock is engraved with scroll ornament, and has the perforated disc to the cock. Signed IOHN: CAMPBELL (Doune). The barrel is fluted at the breech and has an octagonal muzzle, slightly bell-mouthed. It is engraved with scroll ornament in places. The stock is elaborately ornamented with interlacing scrolls executed in engraving and silver inlay. The belt hook is pierced and engraved. The butt is flat, with a scroll terminal. The picker is wanting, but would match the trigger, which has a silver ball terminal. First quarter of XVIIIth century.

Length, 14⅜ in.

The property of N. R. Colville, Esq., F.S.A.Scot.

25. PISTOL, wholly of steel, with flint-lock. The lock is finely engraved with scroll ornament and signed JOHN CAMPBELL (Doune). The

stock is also finely engraved and inlaid with intertwined scrolls and lines in gold and silver. The butt is flat, inlaid on each side with a gold escutcheon, and finished by a scroll terminal. The trigger and picker terminals are also of gold. The belt hook is pierced, engraved, and inlaid. The barrel is fluted at the breech, and octagonal at the muzzle, which is slightly bell-mouthed at the extremity, and is finely engraved with scroll ornament. This pistol bears in places remains of the original blueing of the surface. Third quarter of XVIIIth century.

Length, 14⅛ in.

The property of N. R. Colville, Esq., F.S.A.Scot.

Note.—Although a very fine example, this pistol is inferior in the balance of its proportions and the quality of its decoration to those earlier examples by Alexander Campbell and John Christie of Doune (Plate VIII, Fig. 29).

26. COSTUME PISTOL of steel, with flint-lock. The lock is engraved with scroll ornament and signed McLEOD. The barrel and stock are acid embossed with thistles, the figure of St. Andrew, etc. The barrel is octagonal at breech and muzzle, which is slightly bell-mouthed and stamped with the Birmingham proof marks. The stock is inlaid on the butt with several narrow crossbands and two escutcheons of silver. The butt is finished by a scroll terminal fitted with a steel picker, having its end in poppy-head form. The trigger has a plain steel knob terminal. The surface retains traces of the original blueing. First quarter of XIXth century.

Length, 12¾ in. Bore, ⅝ in.

The property of N. R. Colville, Esq., F.S.A.Scot.

Note.—McLeod may have been a cutler of that name in Edinburgh, who made Highland accoutrements.

27. COSTUME PISTOL of white composition metal and steel, with flint-lock The lock is of steel, finely engraved with scroll ornament, and signed C. PLAYFAIR, ABERDEEN. The steel barrel, engraved with scrolls, has its breech and muzzle octagonal. The barrel bears the Birmingham proof marks on the under side. The stock is of white composition metal finely engraved with scroll ornament. The butt is flat, finished

by a scroll terminal. The picker terminal is in thistle form, of white metal, and the trigger of steel. About 1825.

    Length, 10¼ in.

    The property of C. E. Whitelaw, Esq., F.S.A.Scot.

    Note.—C. Playfair started business about 1820 and the firm still exists.

28.   PISTOL, wholly of steel, with flint-lock. The lock is finely engraved with scroll ornament and signed T. MURDOCH (Leith). The barrel is fluted at the breech and octagonal at the muzzle, which is bell-mouthed at the extremity, and is finely engraved with scroll ornament. The stock is finely engraved with scroll ornament, and terminates in a lobe-shaped butt inlaid with silver, and has a pierced and fluted belt hook. The trigger terminal has the lower half of silver. Fourth quarter of XVIIIth century.

    Length, 12½ in.

    The property of C. E. Whitelaw, Esq., F.S.A.Scot.

PLATE VIII

29.   PISTOL, wholly of steel, with flint-lock. The lock is finely engraved with scroll ornament, and has the perforated disc to the cock. Signed Ioᴺ. CHRYSTIE DOWN (Doune). The barrel is fluted at the breech and octagonal at the muzzle, which is also bell-mouthed at the extremity. It is finely engraved with scroll ornament. The stock is also finely engraved with scroll ornament. There are interlacing lines of silver inlay on the top of the butt, and on each side of it is an oval silver escutcheon. The trigger and picker terminals are of silver. The belt hook is pierced, engraved, and fluted. Third quarter of XVIIIth century.

    Length, 12½ in.

    The property of A. W. Cox, Esq., F.S.A.Scot.

30.   PISTOL of silver and steel, with flint-lock. The lock is of steel, finely engraved and chiselled with scroll ornament, and signed Ioᴺ CHRISTIE,

O

STIRLING. The barrel is of steel, fluted at the breech, and octagonal at the muzzle, which is bell-mouthed at the extremity. The surface is completely engraved with fine scroll ornament. The stock is of silver, finely engraved with scroll ornament, the crowned thistle, etc., and inlaid with interlacing lines and scrolls in gold. Underneath the belt hook is the inscription: TOTUM HOC OPUS SUA MANU PERFECIT JOANNES CHRISTIE. (John Christie executed all this work by his own hand.) The butt is flat, finished by a scroll terminal, and inlaid with a gold escutcheon on either side. The one bears the royal arms of Great Britain, the other bears the royal cypher G.R.IIId., both surmounted by the crown and surrounded by the garter and motto. The belt hook is of steel, engraved, fluted, and delicately pierced with the crowned thistle, etc. The ramrod is also of steel. The trigger and picker terminals and the ramrod tube are of gold.

This pistol may be looked upon as the finest piece of Scottish gunsmith work extant. Third quarter of XVIIIth century.

Length, 12 in.

Preserved in the Royal Armoury, Windsor.

Note.—King George III ascended the throne in 1760, and the pistol was probably presented to him about that time or not long thereafter.

The writer of these notes begs to express his sincere thanks to the owners of the firearms illustrated in the following plates for their kind permission to take photographs for this purpose.

PLATE I

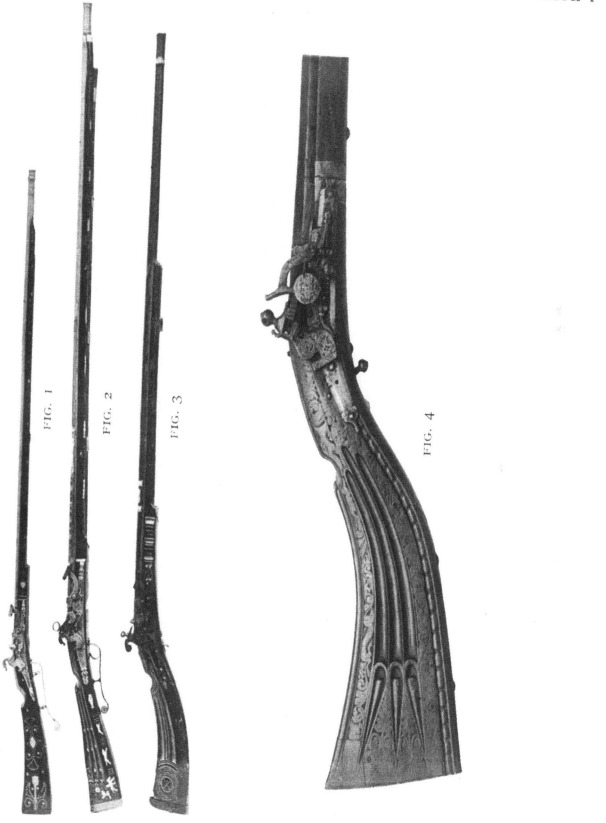

FIG. 1

FIG. 2

FIG. 3

FIG. 4

PLATE II

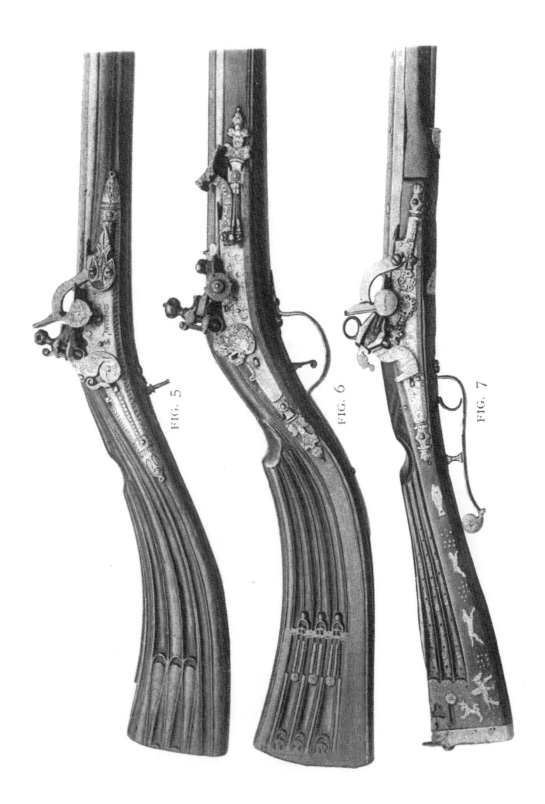

FIG. 5

FIG. 6

FIG. 7

PLATE III

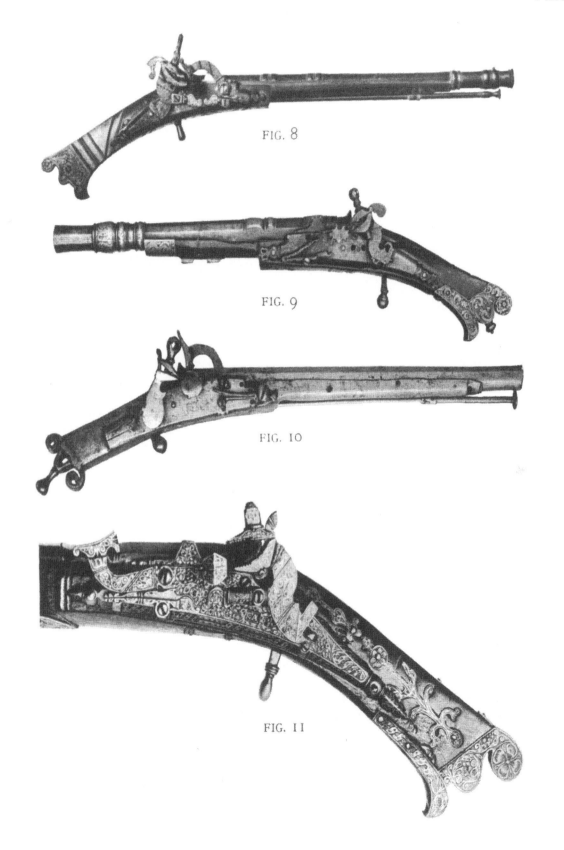

FIG. 8

FIG. 9

FIG. 10

FIG. 11

PLATE IV

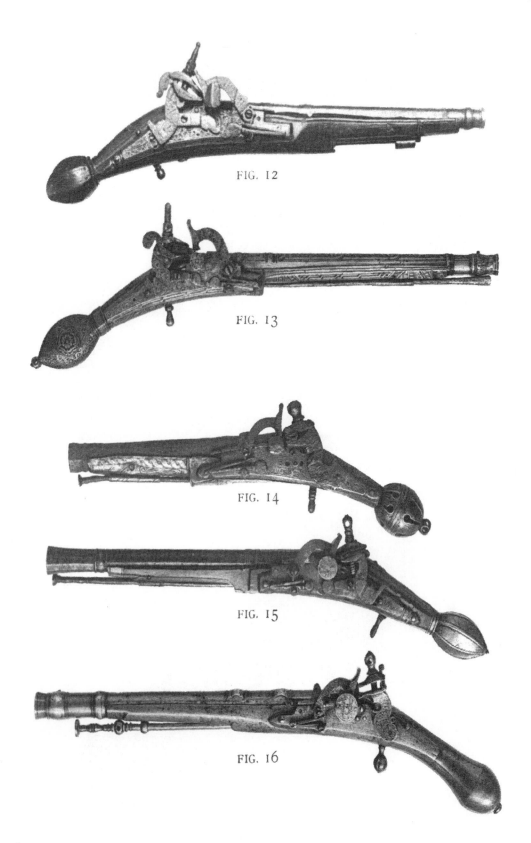

FIG. 12

FIG. 13

FIG. 14

FIG. 15

FIG. 16

PLATE V

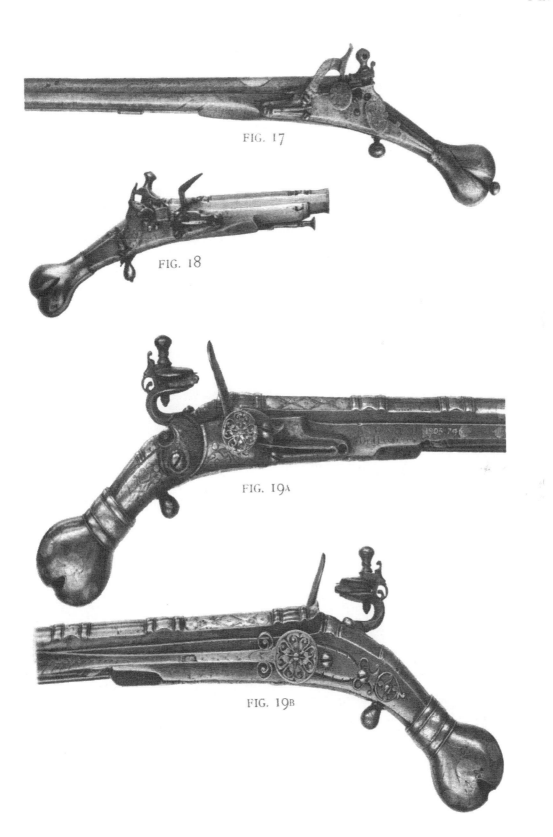

FIG. 17

FIG. 18

FIG. 19A

FIG. 19B

PLATE VI

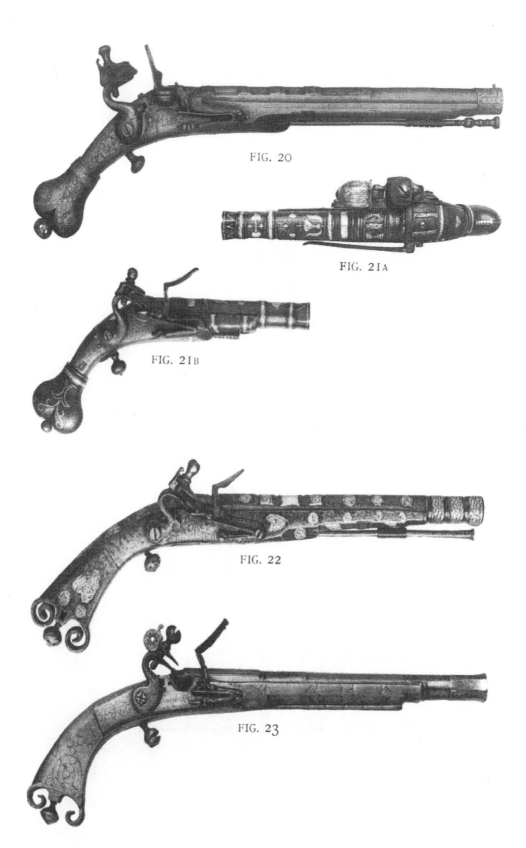

FIG. 20

FIG. 21A

FIG. 21B

FIG. 22

FIG. 23

PLATE VII

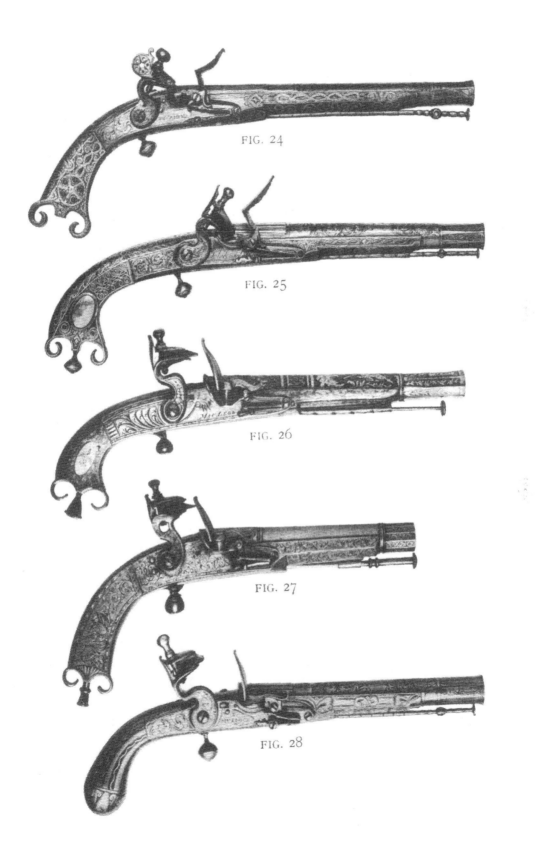

FIG. 24

FIG. 25

FIG. 26

FIG. 27

FIG. 28

PLATE VIII

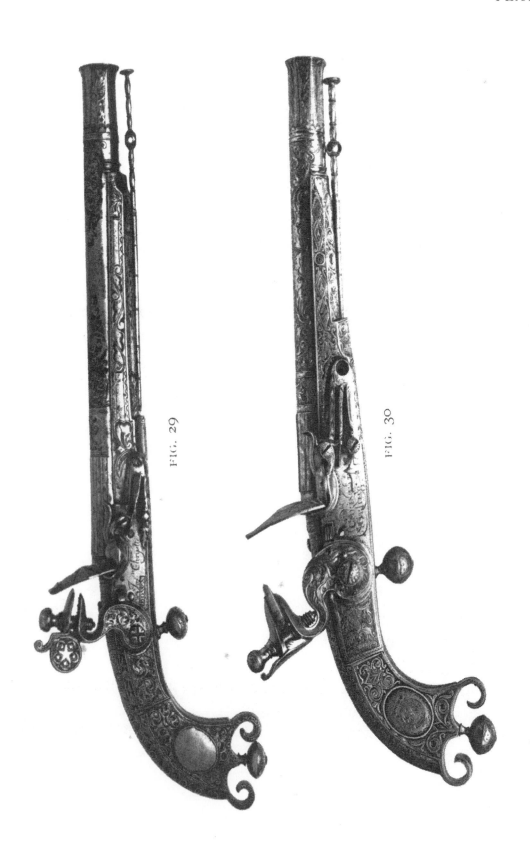

FIG. 29

FIG. 30

MAKERS OF SCOTTISH FIREARMS

Signatures found on Firearms of the XVIth to XVIIIth Centuries

CA 1619.

   Pistol with snaphaunce lock, wood stock, and fish-tail butt. In the Armoury of the Tower, London. (Plate III, Fig. 11.)

IA 1613.

   Pair of Pistols with snaphaunce locks, metal stocks, and globose butts, engraved and gilt. In the Royal Armoury, Stockholm; also on a snaphaunce lock in the Musée d'Artillerie, Paris.

R.A. 1614.

   On a small Arquebus with snaphaunce lock. In the Armoury of the Tower, London. (Plate I, Fig. 1.)

WILL ALLAN

   Pair of steel Pistols with flint-locks and scroll butts, about 1800. Belonging to N. R. Colville, Esq., F.S.A.Scot.

ɓ (J.B.) 1613.

   Pistol with snaphaunce lock, brass stock, and fish-tail butt. In the Zeughaus, Berlin. (Similar to Plate III, Fig. 8.)

W. (WILLIAM) BRYDON. Edinburgh.

   Pistol with flint-lock and walnut stock. Last quarter of the XVIIIth century, belonging to C. E. Whitelaw, Esq., F.S.A.Scot. This maker appears in the Edinburgh Directory of 1800.

JOHN BURGES. Elgin.

   Pistol of steel with flint-lock and heart-shaped butt, about 1700. In the Rotunda Museum, Woolwich.
   Gun with late snaphaunce lock (no date). Belonging to the Countess of Seafield.

AC 1634.

Pair of brass PISTOLS with snaphaunce locks and globose butts. In Aberdeen University Museum. (Plate IV, Fig. 13.)

A'C Pair of steel PISTOLS with flint-locks and scroll butts. Latter half of XVIIIth century, in the Scottish National Museum of Antiquities, Edinburgh.

EC 1627.

PISTOL with snaphaunce lock and metal stock. In the Museum of Sigmaringen, Wurtemburg.

IC

PISTOL with snaphaunce lock, brass stock, and globose butt, about 1650. In Kelvingrove Museum, Glasgow. (Plate IV, Fig. 14.)

WC

PISTOL with flint-lock, brass stock, and scroll butt. Middle of XVIIIth century, belonging to Capt. H. W. Murray, F.S.A., F.S.A.Scot.

THOMAS CADDELL. 1678. Doune.

PISTOL of steel with early flint-lock and scroll butt. In the Museum, Neuchâtel, Switzerland. There were evidently several generations of craftsmen of this name. The first of them is said to have come from Muthill to Doune about 1640, and the last was living in the fourth quarter of the XVIIIth century. *See* " The Statistical Account of Scotland," 1798, vol. 20, p. 86. (Page 67, Fig. E, and Plate VI, Fig. 22.)

ROBERT CADDELL. Doune.

PISTOL of steel with flint-lock and scroll butt. Middle of XVIIIth century, in the Royal Scottish Museum, Edinburgh. A Robert Caddell, brother to Thomas Caddell, appears as a witness to a baptism in 1764.

ALEXANDER CAMERON.

PISTOL of steel with flint-lock and scroll butt. First quarter of XVIIIth century, belonging to N. R. Colville, Esq., F.S.A.Scot. The *Caledonian Mercury* of 15 April 1725 advertised the loss of a pistol by this maker.

JOHN CAMPBELL. Doune.

PISTOL of steel with flint-lock and scroll butt, about 1700. Belonging to Alfred W. Cox, Esq., F.S.A.Scot. There were three generations of pistol makers in this family: the first was an apprentice of the first Thomas Caddell, and the last retired from business shortly before 1798. *See* "The Statistical Account of Scotland," 1798, vol. 20, p. 86. (Plate VII, Figs. 24 and 25.)

ALEXANDER CAMPBELL. Doune.

PISTOL of steel with flint-lock and scroll butt. Middle of XVIIIth century, belonging to C. E. Whitelaw, Esq., F.S.A.Scot.

JAMES CHRISTIE. Perth.

PISTOL of steel with flint-lock and scroll butt. Belonging to A. W. Cox, Esq., F.S.A.Scot. Christie was Deacon of the Hammermen 1771-1772 and 1794-1799.

JOHN CHRISTIE. Doune.

Pair of PISTOLS of steel with flint-locks and scroll butts. Middle of XVIIIth century, belonging to A. W. Cox, Esq., F.S.A.Scot. (Plate VIII, Fig. 29.) *See* following entry.

JOHN CHRISTIE. Stirling.

PISTOL with silver stock, flint-lock, and scroll butt. Third quarter of XVIIIth century, in the Royal Armoury, Windsor. (Plate VIII, Fig. 30.) This may be the same man who worked in Doune earlier.

Æ (AD).

Pair of PISTOLS with snaphaunce locks, brass stocks, and globose butts. Middle of XVIIth century, in the Zeughaus, Berlin.

AD

PISTOL with flint-lock and walnut stock. Middle of XVIIIth century, belonging to C. E. Whitelaw, Esq., F.S.A.Scot. (Page 67, Fig. H.)

FD

PISTOL of steel with flint-lock and heart-shaped butt. First quarter of XVIIIth century, belonging to C. E. Whitelaw, Esq., F.S.A.Scot.

DAVID DUNBAR.

Pair of steel PISTOLS with flint-locks and scroll butts. End of XVIIIth century, in the Royal Scottish Museum, Edinburgh.

EWEN.

Single-barrel GUN with flint-lock. Fourth quarter of XVIIIth century, belonging to C. E. Whitelaw, Esq., F.S.A.Scot.

AL FORBES. 1685. Elgin.

PISTOL of steel with snaphaunce lock and heart-shaped butt; belonging to N. R. Colville, Esq., F.S.A.Scot.

ALEXANDER FORBES.

PISTOL of steel with flint-lock and scroll butt. Latter half of XVIIIth century; belonging to the Marquis of Bute.

JOHN FRASER. 1705. Inverness.

Heavy wall GUN with flint-lock; belonging to the Countess of Seafield.

AG 1622.

Pair of PISTOLS with snaphaunce locks, brass stocks, and fish-tail butts. In the Zeughaus, Berlin.

DH

PISTOL of steel with flint-lock and heart-shaped butt, about 1700. In the Royal Scottish Museum, Edinburgh. (Plate V, Fig. 19.)

HH (I.H.). 1615.

PISTOL with snaphaunce lock, wood stock, and fish-tail butt. In the Museum, Dresden.

IH

PISTOL of steel with flint-lock and heart butt. First quarter of XVIIIth century, belonging to C. E. Whitelaw, Esq., F.S.A.Scot.

WILLIAM HERIOT. Edinburgh.

Single barrel GUN with flint-lock. Third quarter of XVIIIth century, belonging to C. E. Whitelaw, Esq., F.S.A.Scot. This maker appears in the Edinburgh Directory of 1773, and died in that year.

W. HUNTER. Stirling.

PISTOL of steel with flint-lock and scroll butt. Second quarter of XVIIIth century, belonging to A. W. Cox, Esq., F.S.A.Scot.

FRANCIS INNES. Edinburgh. Maker to His Majesty.

Single-and double-barrel GUNS with flint-locks. Third quarter of XVIIIth century, belonging to C. E. Whitelaw, Esq., F.S.A.Scot. This maker appears in the Edinburgh Directory of 1773.

INNES & WALLACE. Edinburgh. "Gunmakers to His Majesty."
Pair of PISTOLS of steel with flint-locks and scroll butts, presented to the Prince of Wales in 1800. In the Royal Armoury, Windsor. This firm appears in the Edinburgh Directory of 1800.

I†K 1598.
Pair of PISTOLS with snaphaunce locks, wood stocks, and fish-tail butts. In the Museum, Dresden.

KENNEDY. Kilmarnock.
POWDER TESTER, with flint-lock, about 1800. Belonging to C. E. Whitelaw, Esq., F.S.A.Scot.

IL 1614.
Pair of brass PISTOLS with snaphaunce locks and globose butts. Formerly in the Morgan Williams collection. Another similar, with this signature, dated 1629, is in the Royal Armoury, Stockholm. Mr. N. R. Colville possesses a third example dated 1617, wholly of brass with a fish-tail butt.

AM 1611.
PISTOL with snaphaunce lock, wood stock, and fish-tail butt. In the Museum, Dresden.

AM
GUN with snaphaunce lock. Second quarter of XVIIth century, belonging to the Countess of Seafield. The signature is uncertain.

AM
Steel PISTOL with flint-lock and heart-shaped butt. Close of XVIIth century, in the Antiquarian Museum, Perth.

MM 1621.
PISTOL of brass with snaphaunce lock and globose butt. Belonging to N. R. Colville, Esq., F.S.A.Scot.

MM (MM)
PISTOL with snaphaunce lock, wood stock, and fish-tail butt. Middle of XVIIth century, in the Royal Scottish Museum, Edinburgh. (Plate III, Fig. 9.) The first letter is not quite clear.

RM 1625.

PISTOL with snaphaunce lock, wood stock, and globose butt. Belonging to C. E. Whitelaw, Esq., F.S.A.Scot. There is another somewhat similar by this maker, dated 1630, in the Schwarzburg, Thuringia.

WM 1673.

On a GUN with snaphaunce lock. Belonging to the Countess of Seafield.

McALLAN

PISTOL of steel with flint-lock and scroll butt. Middle of XVIIIth century, belonging to N. R. Colville, Esq., F.S.A.Scot.

CHARLES McCULLOCH. Inverness.

PISTOL with steel stock and brass barrel, flint-lock and scroll-butt. First quarter of XVIIIth century, belonging to Mrs. Ewing.

DAVID McKENZIE. Dundee.

PISTOL of steel with flint-lock and heart-shaped butt. First quarter of XVIIIth century, in the Albert Institute, Dundee. (Plate VI, Fig. 21.) David McKenzie was admitted to the Hammermen Craft in 1707, and died previous to 1728.

JAMES McKENZIE. Dundee.

PISTOL of steel with flint-lock and heart-shaped butt. Second quarter of XVIIIth century, belonging to C. E. Whitelaw, Esq., F.S.A.Scot. James McKenzie was the eldest son of David McKenzie, Dundee (above), and was admitted to the Hammermen Craft in 1728.

IA. MK. (JAMES McKENZIE). Brechin.

PISTOL of steel with heart butt, and another with scroll butt. Second quarter of XVIIIth century, in the Scottish National Museum of Antiquities, Edinburgh. The stone lintel of McKenzie's shop door or window, carved with his name, a musket, and a pair of holster pistols, is built into the front of a house in Market Street, Brechin.

PATRICK McNAB.

PISTOL of steel with flint-lock and scroll butt. Second quarter of XVIIIth century, belonging to McDougall of McDougall. This maker may be one of the family of hereditary armourers who worked at Dalmally.

J. McROSTY.

PISTOL of steel with flint-lock and scroll butt. First quarter of XVIIIth century, belonging to N. R. Colville, Esq., F.S.A.Scot.

WILLIAM MANN. Glasgow.

Pair of pocket PISTOLS with flint-locks and walnut stocks. Fourth quarter of XVIIIth century, belonging to C. E. Whitelaw, Esq., F.S.A.Scot. He must have worked in Gorbals, then immediately adjoining Glasgow, as his name does not appear among the Hammermen of Glasgow.

JA. MICHIE.

PISTOL of steel with flint-lock and scroll butt. Middle of XVIIIth century, belonging to T. W. Dewar, Esq.

IO. MITCHEL.

PISTOL of brass with flint-lock and heart-shaped butt. Second quarter of XVIIIth century, in the Scottish National Museum of Antiquities, Edinburgh.

ALEXANDER MURDOCH.

Pistol of steel with flint-lock and lobe-shaped butt. Second half of XVIIIth century, in the Scottish National Museum of Antiquities, Edinburgh.

JOHN MURDOCH. Doune.

PISTOL of steel with flint-lock and scroll butt. Latter half of XVIIIth century, in the Scottish National Museum of Antiquities, Edinburgh. He was still working in 1798 (*see* "The Statistical Account of Scotland," 1798, vol. 20, p. 86), and is the maker of several fine pairs of pistols with "cannon" barrels and gilt brass stocks, signed MURDOCH (*see* Catalogue of the Royal Armoury, Windsor).

THOMAS MURDOCH. Leith.

PISTOL of steel with flint-lock and lobe-shaped butt. In South Kensington Museum, London. Another pistol bears on the escutcheon the date 1784. Although the South Kensington pistol is marked LEITH his name does not appear in the Directory of Leith for 1773 or 1800 (the only surviving issues of the Directory up to 1800)

I.O.

Pair of PISTOLS with steel stocks, flint-locks, and heart-shaped butts. First quarter of XVIIIth century, belonging to Elliot M. S. McKirdy, Esq., F.S.A.Scot.

A.P. 1635.

GUN with snaphaunce lock. Belonging to the Countess of Seafield. (Plate I, Fig. 2.)

JAMES PATERSON.

Pair of PISTOLS of steel with right- and left-hand flint-locks and lobe-shaped butts. Fourth quarter of XVIIIth century.

JO. PETCAIRN.

PISTOL of steel with flint-lock and scroll butt. Third quarter of XVIIIth century. On a single-barrel flint-lock gun belonging to C. E. Whitelaw, F.S.A.Scot.

$ (IS) 1684. Inverness.

GUN with snaphaunce lock. Belonging to the Countess of Seafield. (Plate II, Fig. 5.) This signature also appears on the rifled barrel, dated 1667, of a similar piece. (*See* I.T.)

ANDREW SCOTT. Edinburgh (?).

PISTOL of steel with heart-shaped butt. In the Museum, Dresden.

JAMES SCOTT. Edinburgh.

Pair of PISTOLS with flint-locks and walnut stocks. Third quarter of XVIIIth century, belonging to C. E. Whitelaw, Esq., F.S.A.Scot. This maker appears in the Edinburgh Directory of 1773.

IO. SHIEL.

PISTOL of steel with flint-lock and scroll butt. Latter half of XVIIIth century.

ALEXANDER SHIRES. 1700. Old Meldrum.

Pair of PISTOLS of steel with flint-locks and heart-shaped butts. In the Royal Scottish Museum, Edinburgh. (Plate VI, Fig. 20).

GULIELMUS SMITH. 1674. Castle Grant, Grantown.

> On a snaphaunce GUN belonging to the Countess of Seafield and pre-
> served in the armoury at Castle Grant, where there is another signed
> piece by this maker, on which he gives his locus as "Bellachastel"
> (Plate II, Fig. 6), which is the old name for Castle Grant. Smith
> was evidently the family armourer.

GS   1675.

> GUN with snaphaunce lock.
> 1686.
> GUN with snaphaunce lock. (Plate I, Fig. 4.)

WS   1672.

> GUN with snaphaunce lock.
> PISTOL of steel with snaphaunce lock and heart-shaped butt. (Another
> similar specimen is shown in Plate V, Fig. 17.)

> The firearms described in the three immediately preceding items appear
> to be by the same maker—"Gulielmus," or William, Smith. They
> are in the armoury at Castle Grant.

DANIEL STEUART. 1690.

> PISTOL of steel with flint-lock (dog-lock) and scroll butt. In the
> Antiquarian Museum, Perth.

IO. STUART. 1701.

> Pair of PISTOLS of steel with flint-locks and heart-shaped butts.
> Belonging to the Countess of Seafield.

ANDREW STRACHAN. Edzell.

> PISTOL of steel with flint-lock and heart-shaped butt. First quarter
> of XVIIIth century, in the Zeughaus, Berlin.

JAMES SUTHERLAND.

> PISTOL of steel with flint-lock and scroll butt. Belonging to the
> Earl of Ancaster.

I.T.   1671.

> ~~Breechloading~~ RIFLE with snaphaunce lock. Belonging to the
> Countess of Seafield. ~~(Plate I, Fig. 4.)~~ Not illustrated

A.W.   1670.

   PISTOL of steel with early flint-lock (dog-lock) and scroll butt. In the Royal Armoury, Stockholm.

DANIEL WALKER.   Dumbarton.

   PISTOL of steel with flint-lock and lobe-shaped butt. Belonging to C. E. Whitelaw, Esq., F.S.A.Scot.

Note.—Mr. Whitelaw will feel greatly indebted for any further information regarding names found on Scottish Firearms.

LONDON: CHARLES WHITTINGHAM AND GRIGGS (PRINTERS), LTD.
CHISWICK PRESS, TOOKS COURT, CHANCERY LANE.

Printed in Great Britain
by Amazon

22063234R00115